STUDY GUIDE TO ACCOMPANY CHILDREN MOVING:

A REFLECTIVE APPROACH TO TEACHING PHYSICAL EDUCATION

MELISSA PARKER
Ohio State University

GEORGE GRAHAM
University of Georgia

Mayfield Publishing Company

International Standard Book Number: 0-87484-562-9

Manufactured in the United States of America
Mayfield Publishing Company
285 Hamilton Avenue
Palo Alto, California 94301

CONTENTS

ACKNOWLEDGMENTS

Having finished this Study Guide, we wish to express our thanks to those who supported us along the way—some knowingly, others unknowingly.

First, to our students, many of them in elementary physical education classes at the Ohio State University and the University of Georgia, who have put up with several revisions of this work, told us when questions were bad and activities ridiculous. They again have taught us the meaning of reflective teaching, just as children have.

A heartfelt thank you is extended to the staff at Mayfield Publishing Company for their support and work. We thank C. Lansing Hays for believing in the idea from the beginning and for continued suggestions and comments. We are grateful to Judith Ziajka for her supervision of the editing.

That Carole Shockley, our typist, deciphered our virtually illegible handwriting and produced the typescript so quickly is nothing short of a miracle. To her, too, we wish to express our thanks.

MAP
GMG

TO THE STUDENT

Children Moving describes an approach to physical education that is different from the approach many of us experienced when we were in elementary school. It is often difficult to understand something that we have not experienced first hand. Thus one of the major purposes of this Study Guide is to deepen and broaden your understanding of children's physical education beyond what can be gained by simply reading a book. It is one thing to read about teaching. To actually utilize teaching skills is something else.

Another, and more obvious, purpose of the Study Guide is to help you understand the written material more thoroughly. Your teacher for the course will provide you with specific assignments related to the Study Guide, but that doesn't mean that you can't do unassigned activities on your own. Our hope is that you will want to go beyond simply making a good grade in the course and will want to become the best teacher of children's physical education that you can.

HOW TO USE THIS STUDY GUIDE

Each chapter in *Children Moving* has a corresponding chapter in the Study Guide. The Study Guide chapters are divided into four types of activities preceded by a major objective, which will provide you with an understanding of the overall intent or purpose of the chapter.

Each chapter in the Study Guide begins with a section entitled "Reading Comprehension Questions." These questions will help you identify and understand the major points and ideas in the chapter. We recommend that you answer them in your own words rather than simply copying an answer from the textbook. This will enhance your understanding of the material. If you copy from the textbook, your "knowledge" will tend to fail you when you are called on to apply the material.

"Using Your Head" is the title of the second section of each chapter in the Study Guide. These questions will cause you to assimilate ideas contained in the chapter. Don't spend time looking in *Children Moving* for specific answers to these questions. They aren't there. The answers derive from what you have read and depend on your ability to synthesize materials and combine ideas. Many of the "using your head" questions require your opinion, so don't be afraid to create your own ideas based on your reading.

"Field Activities" make up the third section of each chapter in the Study Guide. The aim of these activities is to provide you with actual experiences teaching, observing, and using ideas and suggestions from the textbook. Many of the activities are practical experiences that involve observing or teaching children.

Before scheduling any field activities, please be certain to check with your teacher about appropriate procedures for obtaining permission to observe or teach in a school or other educational agency. Each year, schools in particular receive many requests from individuals who want to observe or work with their children. Consequently, they often have rather elaborate procedures for obtaining permission to "work" in the schools. Your instructor will be aware of these procedures. Although not mentioned specifically in the Study Guide, observations that you make in schools or recreation departments will always require prior approval. The best general guideline is to *always* obtain permission. Never assume that it will be all right for you to stop by and watch a class or two.

Here are a few suggestions about how to conduct observations:

1. Obtain permission ahead of time from the person in charge. If two or three of you plan to visit at once, one person call for all of you so as to avoid three separate telephone calls.
2. Find out what times are convenient for your visit. Be sure to arrive and leave on time.
3. Try not to distract from the ongoing class situation. Find out how the staff generally dresses and dress accordingly. Avoid interacting with the children unless interaction is part of the observation. Make yourself as unobtrusive as possible. The reasons for this are many. First, children are very responsive to visitors, and once a visitor responds to them interaction usually occurs. Then it is impossible for the observer to see a typical setting. Second, interaction with children may be disruptive to the setting, the teacher, and the children themselves. To reduce some of the curiosity of the children, the teacher may want to introduce you with one or two sentences and describe your purpose and the fact that you are busy and not to be disturbed.
4. Always thank those involved for letting you observe.

It has been found that when students follow these guidelines they are welcomed back.

One other word of caution: Quite often in the field activities we have asked that you visit a local elementary school. We have used that term in a generic sense, for we realize it is not always possible to find an elementary school to visit. Some alternatives to visiting an elementary school are a recreation center (public or private), children playing in yards, daycare centers (on or off campus), and university classes in physical education. Use what you can find.

The final section in each Study Guide chapter is entitled "Self-Testing Activities." These activities are designed to help you gain a practical understanding of the material in the textbook and, in many instances, discover things about yourself as a mover.

GENERAL STUDY PROCEDURES

There are several procedures that you may find helpful for enhancing your understanding of the material in *Children Moving*. Actually, these study procedures relate to any course, not only this one. We recommend the following:

1. Before reading a chapter in the textbook, read the questions for that chapter in the Study Guide. This will give you a general understanding of the important ideas to be understood in your reading.

2. Read the chapter from beginning to end without a break.

3. Write out the answers to the reading comprehension and "using your head" questions. It will be tempting to answer the questions mentally or simply underline the important passages in the textbook. If you succumb to that temptation, however, you will not learn as much or as quickly. The material in each chapter may serve as a supplement to a lecture or class discussion, or it may be new information.

We realize that you may use a different set of procedures to help you learn. Don't change your method if it is successful. Our suggestions are simply recommendations that have worked for many.

We hope that the Study Guide will enable you to further understand the value of physical education for children while simultaneously helping you on your way to becoming a reflective teacher. Work hard—we wish you well!

CHAPTER 1
REFLECTIVE TEACHING

pp. 5–12

OBJECTIVE

After reading Chapter 1 of *Children Moving* for the second time, you should be able to answer these questions and complete the activities related to reflective teaching in physical education.

READING COMPREHENSION QUESTIONS

1. What is meant by a "linear approach" to teaching?

2. What is reflective teaching? What are its basic characteristics?

3. What is effective teaching?

4. What is meant by "invariant" teaching?

5. What factors might contribute to the dissimilarity of teaching situations?

6. What are some of the differences between children of low and high socioeconomic status?

7. Why and how would class size affect teaching?

8. What is one difference between experienced teachers and nonexperienced teachers that allows the former to teach reflectively?

9. What is discipline?

USING YOUR HEAD

1. What philosophical assumptions do the authors make about children, about teachers, and about different teaching environments?

2. Define "generic."

3. What is meant by the statement that "teaching is situational rather than generic" (see page 6 of *Children Moving*)?

4. Describe the difference in your subject area between an invariant and a reflective teacher with regard to curriculum.

5. Give one example of how equipment, or the lack of it, can affect teaching situations.

6. Can one learn to discipline classes or is maintaining order an inborn ability?

7. In your own words explain the major implication of reflective teaching.

FIELD ACTIVITIES

1. Think of two elementary schools that you are fairly familiar with. Name each one and, in the space provided, list ways in which they are similar. Then list differences. Consider curricular, physical, philosophical, and other factors.

School 1: _____   School 2: _____

Similarities

Differences

2. For about ten minutes, observe two young children playing together. List the similarities and differences that you see.

Activity observed: _____

When: _____

Where: _____

Approximate age of children: _____

Child 1	Child 2
Similarities	
Differences	

3. Think of two elementary school teachers whom you know. List their similarities and then their differences.

Teacher 1	Teacher 2
Similarities	
Differences	

4. Visit two elementary schools. Write out an equipment inventory for each.

School 1	School 2

5. Observe two elementary school teachers. What are the similarities and differences in the ways they handle discipline problems?

Teacher 1	Teacher 2
Similarities	
Differences	

SELF-TESTING ACTIVITIES

1. Go back to all five of the field activities and, with a partner or small group, list any implications you can draw about the teaching of physical education in the various settings. After you finish, you might want to refer to Table 1.1, Figure 1.1, and pages 6 to 11 of *Children Moving* to check some of the variables that affect teaching.

2. Refer to field activity 1 and, with a small group, decide what reflective teaching would look like in each school.

3. Refer to field activity 4. With a partner list activities that you can imagine being available to you if you taught a class of thirty in each school.

School 1	School 2

CHAPTER 2
TEACHING BY SKILL THEMES

pp. 13–21

OBJECTIVE

After reading Chapter 2 of *Children Moving* for the second time, you should
be able to answer these questions and complete the activities related to
skill themes and apply the material in your planning of elementary physical
education activities.

READING COMPREHENSION QUESTIONS

1. What needs to be taught in physical education before a game is taught?
    Why?

2. What is teaching by themes?

3. What is a theme?

4. What is the schema theory? How does it provide support for teaching
    by themes?

5.   What are skill themes?

6.   What are movement concepts? How do they modify skill themes?

7.   Define the three categories of skill themes. What skills are included in each category?

8.   Define the three general categories of movement concepts.

9.   Into what areas is each movement concept subdivided?

10.   How can concepts modify other concepts?

11.   How can you distinguish skill themes from concepts?

12.   Why and when are movement concepts taught as skill themes?

13.   How are simple and complex skill themes taught?

14. What does the spiral indicate about skill development?

15. What is meant by "revisiting" themes?

16. Why would children regress to a lower skill level when the context of a movement is varied?

USING YOUR HEAD

1. How are variety and diversity in skill themes accomplished?

2. Why would one want to teach by skill themes?

3. Describe Figure 2.1 (page 16 in *Children Moving*) in your own words.

4. What major skill themes relate generally to games? To dance? To gymnastics?

5. How could the concept of "direction" be used in games? In dance? In gymnastics?

FIELD ACTIVITIES

1. Take two manila folders and make a skill theme wheel as described on
    pages 16 and 17 of *Children Moving*. It helps if you color each cate-
    gory of skill themes and movement concepts with a different color.
    (Hint: Movement concepts are described in forty-one spaces on the out-
    side of the wheel.)

2. Go to a local playground, park, or backyard. For five minutes watch a
    group of children play. What skill themes do you see?

    Place: _____

    Date: _____

    Time: _____

    Number of children: _____

    Approximate age: _____

    Skill themes: _____

    _____

    _____

    _____

    _____

3. Find three pictures of three different game activities (for example,
    football, baseball, and basketball). Attach all three. List all
    similarities in themes and concepts that occur in all of the pictures.

             Skill Themes   Movement Concepts

    _____   _____

    _____   _____

    _____   _____

    _____   _____

    _____   _____

    _____   _____

4. Find pictures of a gymnastics skill, a game skill, and a dance skill.
    Attach all three. List all similarities in themes and concepts that
    occur in the pictures.

Skill Themes	Movement Concepts
_____	_____
_____	_____
_____	_____
_____	_____
_____	_____

SELF-TESTING ACTIVITIES

1. Find a picture of a sport skill and attach it to this page. Then take the picture and describe it in skill theme terms, using the following format. The clearer the picture, the easier it will be to describe. Isolated action shots work best. You may want to use Table 2.2 and Figure 2.1 in *Children Moving* to check your work.

   Major skill involved: _____

   Is the skill locomotor, nonlocomotor, or manipulative? _____

List any secondary skill themes involved.	Locomotor, Nonlocomotor, or Manipulative?
_____	_____
_____	_____
_____	_____

Movement concepts involved as modifiers and aspects of each concept:

Space

Location: _____

Direction: _____

Level: _____

Pathway: _____

Extension: _____

Effort

Time: _____

Force: _____

Flow: _____

<u>Relationships</u>

Of body parts: _____

_____

_____

With objects and/or people: _____

_____

_____

With people: _____

_____

_____

2. On the basis of your answers to field activity 3, what skill themes and
    modifiers could you use to teach generic game skills that would be
    applicable to all three games that you picked? Go beyond what you see
    in each picture.

           Skill Themes   Movement Concepts

    _____   _____

    _____   _____

    _____   _____

    _____   _____

    _____   _____

3. You have been given the skill theme of throwing. Identify five ways in
    which you can vary the context of the theme to make it more challenging.

    a. _____

    b. _____

    c. _____

    d. _____

    e. _____

4. With a partner, pick any skill theme and add movement concepts to make
    a progression from simple to complex. Brainstorm your way through.
    There is no one right answer.

Skill theme: _____ Simple

Movement concepts: _____

_____

_____

_____

_____

_____

_____

_____ Complex

CHAPTER 3
PLANNING

pp. 25–39

OBJECTIVE

After reading Chapter 3 of *Children Moving* for the second time, you should
be able to answer these questions and complete the activities and have a
better understanding of the need for reflective planning.

READING COMPREHENSION QUESTIONS

1. What are both the long- and the short-term implications of ineffective
    planning?

2. What are some of the factors that influence effective planning? How do
    they affect planning?

3. What three steps are taken in reflective planning? Explain each so
    that you understand it.

4. Why is it important to outline the sequences of lessons to be taught?

5. Where can individual variations be accommodated? Why?

6. How do actual lesson plans evolve? Why is it not feasible to use pre-packaged lesson plans?

7. Explain the four parts to a lesson plan.

8. What is set induction? What is its purpose?

9. What are two purposes for the core of the lesson?

10. What are two purposes for the conclusion of a lesson?

11. What criteria are given for deciding to change activities?

12. What is intratask variation?

13. What ideas does a teacher need to record daily about lessons and why?

14. What is characteristic of an appropriately designed task?

15. What is meant by the concept of "maximum participation"? Why is it important?

16. Planning never seems to be fun. List three things that may make it more enjoyable.

USING YOUR HEAD

1. Why can't an exact recipe for planning be given?

2. In what ways can a teacher determine how responsible a class is?

3. How do children's skill levels and interests affect planning?

4. How is elementary yearly planning different from secondary?

5. Why would one focus on movement concepts more with an inexperienced class?

6. What would happen if one had taught several lessons in a sequence and everything was going wrong? What would happen if one had come to the end of a sequence and things were going superbly well? Make a general statement about planning on the basis of your answers to these two questions.

7. What criteria might determine what ultimately should be presented in a lesson?

8. The guide for planning seems cumbersome and long. Why is all the information stated there needed? What might happen if you didn't include it?

9. The authors suggest that all teachers do not write objectives every day. What comment, however, counters this statement somewhat? What do all successful teachers know?

10. Children often ask, "When do I get to play the game?" What can a teacher do to minimize the number of times this question is asked?

FIELD ACTIVITIES

1. You have an inexperienced class that meets for physical education every school day for 185 days. Using Table 3.1 in *Children Moving*, determine how many days this class would spend in each activity listed. Also determine the percentage of time to be spent in each skill theme and concept.

Movement Concepts	Days	Percentage of Class Meetings
Location	_____	_____
Directions, levels, pathways, and extensions	_____	_____

Movement Concepts—continued	Days	Percentage of Class Meetings
Relationships	_____	_____
Effort	_____	_____
Skill Themes		
Locomotor skills	_____	_____
Throwing, catching, kicking, and punting	_____	_____
Dribbling, volleying, striking	_____	_____
Shapes, turning, twisting, stretching, curling	_____	_____
Balancing, transferring, weight, rolling	_____	_____
Jumping and landing	_____	_____
Total	_____	_____
	185	100%

2. Pick a skill theme and develop, roughly, a sequence of five lessons, based on Table 3.3 in *Children Moving*. (Do not use jumping.)

Skill theme: _____

Lesson Focus

Day 1: _____

_____

Day 2: _____

_____

Day 3: _____

_____

Day 4: _____

_____

Day 5: _____

_____

3. Use the "Guide for Reflective Planning," which follows on page 19. Try to fill in all blanks through "in this lesson I want the children to learn." All data should be fictional but realistic. Make up

something you are comfortable with. Refer to Figure 3.1 in *Children Moving* if you need help.

4. Visit a local elementary school and observe two physical education classes. What skill themes are used in each? What movement concepts are being used?

	Skill Themes	Movement Concepts
Class 1		
Class 2		

5. For the same two classes that you observed in activity 4, see if you can identify the introduction, development, core, and conclusion of the lesson. If one aspect did not occur, simply state that fact.

	Class 1	Class 2
Introduction		
Development		
Core		
Conclusion		

GUIDE FOR REFLECTIVE PLANNING

CLASS NAME _____ CLASS SKILL LEVEL _____

LENGTH (TIME) OF LESSON_____ # OF MEETINGS PER WEEK _____

EQUIPMENT TO BE USED: 1)_____ 2)_____ 3)_____

4)_____ 5)_____

ORGANIZATIONAL PATTERN _____ FACILITY _____

MAJOR SKILL THEME OR MOVEMENT CONCEPT _____

    SUBCONCEPT(S) OF THEME(S) 1)_____

                      2)_____

IN THIS LESSON I WANT THE CHILDREN TO LEARN: _____

    LESSON COMPONENTS   OBSERVATIONAL FOCUS

INTRODUCTION:

DEVELOPMENT:

CORE:

CONCLUSION:

LESSON EVALUATION (USE REVERSE SIDE)

GUIDE FOR REFLECTIVE PLANNING, p. 2

LESSON EVALUATION

    1)   HOW CAN THIS PLAN BE IMPROVED?

    2)   HOW COULD MY TEACHING PERFORMANCE BE IMPROVED?

6. Assume that you have been given this task: "By yourself find as many
    ways to balance as possible. Stay in your own space and try not to
    fall over." Identify five possible intratask variations to the origi-
    nal task.

    a. _____

    _____

    b. _____

    _____

    c. _____

    _____

    d. _____

    _____

    e. _____

    _____

SELF-TESTING ACTIVITIES

Use a partner for all the self-testing activities in this chapter. You will
really have to brainstorm and look ahead to the skill theme chapters to get
ideas. Look back at these ideas at the end of your course. They will probably change dramatically! But that's OK.

1. The purpose of the introduction to a lesson is to provide an initial
    activity to get the class active quickly. The task should relate to
    the day's lesson. Your lesson is dealing with balance on low equip-
    ment. Design an introductory activity for an average control-level
    class.

2. You are introducing a group of skilled children to the idea of running
    to kick. Briefly describe the development stage of a lesson in which
    this skill is introduced.

3. Your class has been studying traveling in different pathways. Design
    the core to a lesson that encompasses this concept.

4. What are two ways to conclude a lesson on striking to different levels
    with different body parts?

5. The observational focus of a lesson helps teachers determine what they
    need to look for while they are teaching. For self-testing activities
    1, 2, and 3, design at least two observational foci.

1.   (a) _____

     (b) _____

2.   (a) _____

     (b) _____

3.   (a) _____

     (b) _____

6. Go back to field activity 3 and try to fill in the remainder of the lesson plan.

CHAPTER 4
CLASS, GROUP, AND INDIVIDUAL INSTRUCTION

pp. 40–52

OBJECTIVE

After reading Chapter 4 of *Children Moving* for the second time, you should be able to answer these questions and complete the activities related to different types of instruction and incorporate the techniques in your teaching.

READING COMPREHENSION QUESTIONS

1. Organizational patterns are generally discussed in terms of a continuum ranging from direct to indirect decision making by the teacher. What does this continuum mean? What is represented by the extremes?

2. What three broad categories can instructional patterns be divided into? Define each. What specific types of instruction are included in each category?

3. What happens to skill performance in a competitive situation? How does this relate to the running of relay races?

4. What is cohort instruction? What are its advantages?

5. What advantages does problem solving or guided discovery have over cohort instruction?

6. What is the difference between guided discovery and problem solving?

7. What are learning centers?

8. What is the difference between recess and an elective?

9. What are task sheets?

10. How would independent contracting work?

11. What is the purpose of an open gym?

12. What two things can be used to determine the organizational pattern of a class?

USING YOUR HEAD

1. What kinds of decisions does the teacher have to make before deciding how to organize for instruction?

2. The authors believe that it is perfectly acceptable to start at the direct end of the continuum. Why is it not acceptable to stay there, if you believe that children are individuals?

3. Why would skill level decrease in a competitive situation if the skill is new to a child?

4. What are the implied advantages of using learning centers?

5. Why is it important for children to be able to design their own activities? Is this an overnight process? How does one help children learn to make decisions?

6. Why wouldn't an "open gym" be a good starting place with a new class?

7. Mainstreaming is required by law in the United States. What organizational pattern would be the easiest way to mainstream a handicapped child into physical education?

8. How does the teaching approach used in a child's classroom affect the teaching approach used in physical education?

FIELD ACTIVITIES

1. Go observe any four classes being taught, preferably physical education classes. What organizational pattern is being used, according to Table 4.2 in *Children Moving*?

	Class	Subject	Organization
1.	_____	_____	_____
2.	_____	_____	_____
3.	_____	_____	_____
4.	_____	_____	_____

2. Go to a school that mainstreams mentally and physically handicapped children into regular physical education classes. Describe what steps are taken to incorporate those children into the regular class.

Child 1: _____

_____

Child 2: _____

_____

Child 3: _____

_____

SELF-TESTING ACTIVITIES

As in Chapter 3, use a partner to help you develop the answers to these activities.

1. You have been working in the area of throwing and catching, and your students are fairly responsible. What four learning centers could you set up to help facilitate this development?

Station 1: _____

_____

Station 2: _____

_____

Station 3: _____

_____

Station 4: _____

_____

2. A task sheet is a series of challenges provided to children so that
    they can practice at their own rate. Design six activities for a task
    sheet on jumping and landing.

    a. _____

    _____

    b. _____

    _____

    c. _____

    _____

    d. _____

    _____

    e. _____

    _____

    f. _____

    _____

3. Using a problem-solving format, design three problems that could be
    used with rolling.

    a. _____

    _____

    b. _____

    _____

    c. _____

    _____

4. Keith is a third-grader. He is quite a well-rounded and active child.
    He wants to participate in everything; yet he has one leg that is

about four inches shorter than the other. On the shorter leg he wears a brace to his hip and a built-up shoe. He comes to class with the rest of the children and does not use crutches. Use the accompanying IEP form (see page 29) to plan Keith's activities in a volleying unit. The annual goals in relation to striking are to (1) strike a ball in the air, determining the speed, direction, and pathway, and (2) strike a ball with a partner, continuously trying to outwit the partner.

5. Go back to field activity 1. What alternative ways can you think of to organize the lessons you saw?

Class 1: _____

Class 2: _____

Class 3: _____

Class 4: _____

6. One of the goals of physical education is to provide maximum participation for all children (Chapter 3). How do the different organizational patterns relate to maximum participation?

INDIVIDUALIZED EDUCATION PROGRAM (IEP)

SCHOOL YEAR _____

STUDENT _____

LEVEL OF FUNCTIONING _____

CLASS _____

EVALUATION PERIOD _____   IEP IMPLEMENTOR _____

TITLE _____

ANNUAL GOALS:

THE STUDENT WILL DEVELOP THE ABILITY TO

1)
2)
3)
4)

SHORT-TERM OBJECTIVES	EXPERIENCE AND/OR TEACHING STRATEGY	EVALUATION	DATE MASTERED

CHAPTER 5
ESTABLISHING
A LEARNING
ENVIRONMENT

pp. 53–58

OBJECTIVE

After reading Chapter 5 of *Children Moving* for the second time, you should be able to answer these questions and complete the activities and go on to develop some guidelines for establishing a learning environment in physical education.

READING COMPREHENSION QUESTIONS

1. What is physical education? What is recess?

2. What is discipline (see Chapter 1 or 6)? How does discipline differ from establishing a learning environment?

3. Define "activity time," "waiting time," and "management time."

4. What are some activities that can be used to teach children to listen in physical education?

5. What are some of the basic ground rules that the authors try to establish for children who are just beginning their physical education experiences? What helps children to understand these rules?

6. What is meant by "critical demandingness" (in your own words)?

USING YOUR HEAD

1. Why is the attitude of the teacher so important to a learning environment?

2. The authors comment that at times it takes several lessons or more to establish a learning environment. Why and when might this happen?

3. How do activity time, waiting time, and management time affect physical education? Relate your answer to the concept of "maximum participation" brought out in Chapter 3.

4. The statement is made on page 55 of *Children Moving* that children need to understand that safety is their responsibility as well as the teacher's. If that attitude is accepted, what implications does it have for students in a class?

FIELD ACTIVITIES

1. You have a second-grade class that is just beginning their experience in physical education. List in detail three activities that could be used at the beginning of each lesson to help the children to listen.

   a. _____

b. _____

c. _____

2. Visit a neighborhood elementary school. Watch children on the playground. Can you tell whether recess or physical education class is occurring? How?

3. Conduct an informal survey. Call at least five elementary schools—two local city, two private, and one in a nearby system. Find out if they have physical education, who teaches it (specialist or classroom teacher), how many times per week, and whether they also have recess. The following chart may help you.

School	P.E.	Teacher	Times/Week	Recess
1.				
2.				
3.				
4.				
5.				

4. Visit four or five local elementary school physical education classes. What signal does each teacher use to get the class to stop and listen?

Teacher	Signal
a. _____	_____
b. _____	_____
c. _____	_____
d. _____	_____
e. _____	_____

5. Children remember things better if they can see them in a positive way constantly. You are a classroom teacher in your major field in a fourth grade. Draft a poster to indicate how you would explain rules for behavior in physical education. Be sure to include your rules. Remember, the more colorful, the better.

SELF-TESTING ACTIVITIES

1. Jason is a six-year-old paraplegic with two nonjointed prostheses. You are working on a throwing and catching unit. Design two activities and indicate how you could use another student to incorporate Jason into class.

    a. _____

    _____

    b. _____

    _____

2. You are a new third-grade teacher in a local school. There is no organized physical education; recess is the substitute. You are determined, at least with your class, to teach physical education. Draft a letter to send home to parents to start to foster proper attitudes toward physical education. Share this letter with your classmates to see what major points were included or excluded.

3. Children love all sorts of challenges, and anything can be a challenge. You have a fifth-grade class that takes forever to put equipment away. Describe in detail a challenge system to increase their promptness at doing such tasks. Remember to include what you would do when their promptness starts to increase. (If you want a technical term for this, you are "shaping" behavior.)

CHAPTER 6
DISCIPLINE

pp. 59–69

OBJECTIVE

After reading Chapter 6 of *Children Moving* for the second time, you should be able to answer these questions and complete the activities pertaining to discipline in the physical education setting.

READING COMPREHENSION QUESTIONS

1. What should be your first step as a teacher when you find the majority of the students in your class misbehaving? Why?

2. What two general guidelines have been found to be effective in disciplining children?

3. What things can be found out by tape-recording your classes?

4. What would be the major point to remember in a person-to-person dialogue with a student?

5.   What is a time-out? How is it used?

6.   When is a time-out not successful?

7.   What is a token system? When does it become unnecessary?

8.   When is a letter to parents used in disciplining a child? What needs
     to be included in the letter?

9.   What two ways have been found to work with whole-class discipline
     problems?

10. How does a class rewards system work?

11. What is a behavior game? How is it played?

12. What are some characteristics of an effective disciplinarian?

USING YOUR HEAD

1. What can be done about children who constantly do not want to partici-
    pate in physical education?

2. Why should sending a child to the principal be a last resort in dis-
    ciplining?

3. Why are behavior games not permanent?

4. What is the difference between "good" and "bad" teachers when it comes
    to discipline?

FIELD ACTIVITIES

1. Go to a local classroom and audio-tape a teacher's class (with permis-
    sion), or listen to a tape provided for you. Listen for the following
    information: (1) What names, if any, are called excessively? (2) What
    children are praised excessively? (3) What children are criticized
    excessively?

2. List five tokens that could be used in physical education.

    a. _____

    b. _____

    c. _____

    d. _____

    e. _____

3. List five free-choice items that could be used in physical education.

    a. _____

    b. _____

c. _____

d. _____

e. _____

4. You have decided to give class rewards for on-task behavior in physical education class. The principal has okayed the idea with the proviso that every class has an equal chance of receiving an award and that no one will be singled out as being the best. What kinds of rewards could be used and how?

Rewards	How Used
a. _____	_____
b. _____	_____
c. _____	_____
d. _____	_____
e. _____	_____

SELF-TESTING ACTIVITIES

1. Go back to field activity 1. What advice could you give the teacher on the basis of the information gathered from the tape?

2. Mike has been a constant problem for you in class. He continually disrupts other children and will not follow directions. You have tried praising him, ignoring him, and even giving him time-outs. Nothing works. You now decide to write a letter to his parents. Draft a letter to send to Mike's parents.

3. Marcie seems to have problems in physical education class. At times she disturbs others and at times she is very antisocial and a loner. You have decided to have a personal conference with her. Describe a fictional dialogue with her.

    Teacher:

    Marcie:

    Teacher:

Marcie:

Teacher:

Marcie:

Teacher:

4. Mrs. Conroy's fifth-grade class has always been perfectly horrible, and
    you have finally "had it." You have tried everything. The children
    come to you the last period of the day and totally ruin even very good
    days. You have decided to use a behavior game with them. The twenty-
    four students are listed below. Design in detail the behavior game you
    will use.

*1.	Jack	*13.	Monica
2.	Alan	**14.	Charlie
3.	Julie	*15.	Chris
4.	Karleen	*16.	Dempsey (girl)
*5.	Randi (girl)	**17.	Carlos
6.	Richard	**18.	Swan (boy)
7.	Matthew	*19.	Tommy
**8.	Bo (boy)	**20.	Robert
*9.	Griff (boy)	*21.	Lee
10.	Courtney	22.	Libby
11.	Rayza (girl)	**23.	Kevin
*12.	Catherine	**24.	Anne

---

   *The best-behaved students.
   **The worst-behaved students.

5. Kevin has been ignoring the stop signal in class and continues to play
    long after the rest of the class is listening. You want to give him a
    time-out. How would you do it? Where would you send him? Explain in
    detail what you would do.

6. You are teaching a fourth-grade class that comes to you twice a week
    for thirty minutes. The classroom teacher is middle-aged but new to
    teaching and fairly weak. Discipline is all but lacking. The stu-
    dents often cut up with you, and you are trying to be very patient.
    But the breaking point arrives when one day in class they throw bean
    bags out the windows. What would you do to try to regain control of
    the class?

7. After you have completed the self-testing activities, find a classmate
    or a small group to discuss your conclusions with you. What different
    ideas emerge? What could you add to your answers? What do you think
    will really work?

CHAPTER 7
OBSERVING, ANALYZING, AND PRESCRIBING

pp. 70–78

OBJECTIVE

After reading Chapter 7 of *Children Moving* for the second time, you should be able to answer these questions and complete the activities relating to observing, analyzing, and prescribing children's movement.

READING COMPREHENSION QUESTIONS

1. What are the four steps to observation and what is the purpose of each?

2. What must be identified in the observation guide?

3. What three things are initially focused on when the class as a whole is observed?

4. What is meant by "back-to-the-wall" technique? When can it be abandoned?

5. How does the scanning technique work?

6. What decisions can be made after data are analyzed?

7. What should the teacher's prescription message to a child contain?

8. What basic steps can you take to learn to observe more effectively?

USING YOUR HEAD

1. Why is observation so important?

2. What needs to be done with the data collected after observation?

3. What is observation analysis? Can it be learned?

4. Why is observation difficult in a teaching situation?

5. What is meant by "knowledge of results" or "statement of results"? Why is it ineffective?

FIELD ACTIVITIES

1. In a college class that you attend, practice scanning. (The professor
    will love it.) About once every ten minutes look up, scan the room,
    and record the number of students "off task." Be sure to record the
    total number of students as well.

    Scan   Off Task/Total Number of Students

       1   _____

       2   _____

       3   _____

       4   _____

       5   _____

2. Using the following observation guide, observe three children or adults
    at play. Watch first one, then another. Do not try to watch all three
    at once. Try to describe their movement. Remember to watch each only
    briefly and describe his or her movement in detail, not in global
    terms. Do not use the words "good," "bad," "right," or "wrong." Use
    movement words instead. Good luck!

	Skill Observed	Description of Movement
Child 1		
Child 2		
Child 3		

3. On page 72 of *Children Moving* there is a list of three things that
    should be done during the initial phases of observation. Go to a local
    physical education class and observe the beginning of class, specifi-
    cally checking for the things listed. Record your observation on the
    accompanying table.

	Yes/No	Comments
Are children working safely?		
Is equipment used properly?		
Is the assigned task appropriate?		

4. Go to a local elementary school or recreation center where children are being taught physical activities. For one class, monitor the teacher's position in class and record it as indicated in the example. Do this about every five minutes. Remember to include the children's positions in your recordings. How many children does the teacher not see?

    x = Child   0 = Teacher   ← = Line of vision

Example

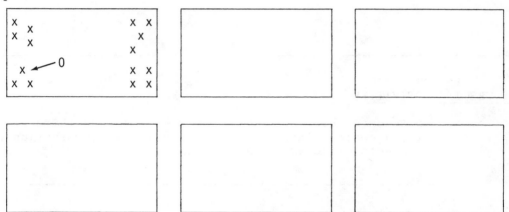

5. Observe a physical education class at a local elementary school. During the class, observe as many children as possible and record movement information about them. Use the format on page 44. Don't be discouraged if you feel you missed a lot. Observation takes practice. Try it again when you are actually teaching.

Theme: _____

Movement concept: _____

Child's Name or Description	Description of Movement

SELF-TESTING ACTIVITIES

1. You are to teach a throwing and catching lesson to a third grade that is basically a control-level class. Formulate an observation guide with five aspects of movement to look for.

    a. _____

    b. _____

    c. _____

    d. _____

    e. _____

2. After you finish, pick five activities on your own and develop observation guides. Remember to identify the skill and the proficiency level, as well as the movement aspects.

    a. Skill: _____

        Proficiency level: _____

        (1) _____

      (2) _____

      (3) _____

      (4) _____

      (5) _____

b. Skill: _____

    Proficiency level: _____

      (1) _____

      (2) _____

      (3) _____

      (4) _____

      (5) _____

c. Skill: _____

    Proficiency level: _____

      (1) _____

      (2) _____

      (3) _____

      (4) _____

      (5) _____

d. Skill: _____

    Proficiency level: _____

      (1) _____

      (2) _____

      (3) _____

      (4) _____

      (5) _____

e. Skill: _____

    Proficiency level: _____

(1) _____

(2) _____

(3) _____

(4) _____

(5) _____

3. Go back to field activity 2. For each child observed, add an analysis
   and prescription. After you finish, check your answers with the criteria listed on pages 74 and 75 of *Children Moving*.

	Analysis	Prescription
Child 1		
Child 2		
Child 3		

4. With a friend, find some children or adults to observe while at play.
   Choose three and observe each one. You and your friend should work
   separately using the following chart. After you have finished, compare
   answers and discuss your differences.

Theme: _____

Movement concepts: _____

Child's Name or Description	Description of Movement	Prescription

CHAPTER 8
EVALUATING STUDENT PROGRESS

pp. 79–89

OBJECTIVE

After reading Chapter 8 of *Children Moving* for the second time, you should be able to answer these questions and complete the activities involving the evaluation of students' progress.

READING COMPREHENSION QUESTIONS

1. What is summative evaluation? Can you give an example?

2. What is formative evaluation? Can you give an example?

3. What do the authors propose that a child be graded on? Why?

4. Describe a checklist. What is on one? How does a checklist help with evaluation and observation?

5. How can individual records be kept? What is their purpose?

6. What can be done if you don't have time to write after every class?

7. What is the function of a "log"? How does it work?

8. How can standardized tests occupy a functional role in physical education classes?

9. What is the difference between grading and evaluation?

10. What is norm-referenced grading?

11. What does a teacher need to tell parents in a progress report?

USING YOUR HEAD

1. How is evaluation used in the "real world"?

FIELD ACTIVITIES

1. Go to a local school and obtain permission from the physical education teacher for you to ask the children to keep journals about physical education for two weeks. At the end of that time, collect and read the journals. Also share them with the teacher.

2. Find a group of children who meet regularly for physical activity of some sort, or use the classroom if such a group is not available. Observe one child for five lessons and use a progress report card to report on his or her progress. (See the example on page 84 of *Children Moving* if you need help.)

3. Obtain from nearby school systems a copy of their report cards for the elementary grades. In what ways is physical education achievement reported to the home?

4. Visit the library, look in physical education texts and measurement books, and try to find a standardized test that your students could use with the skill theme of striking. Xerox and attach.

SELF-TESTING ACTIVITIES

1. From the sequence developed in field activity 2 for Chapter 3, design an individual progress checklist for that skill theme. Refer to page 81 in *Children Moving* to check your work.

2. For the same skill theme you used in activity 1, design a hypothetical report to parents, with the data filled in. Did you include these elements?

    a. Name of child
    b. Theme of study
    c. Brief description of study
    d. Demonstration of theme understanding
    e. Skill level
    f. Group/partner interaction
    g. Additional comments

3. For the field activities you kept a progress report on one child. In Chapter 7 you collected data on several children (see page 46). Now go back and translate that data onto a progress report form.

    Note: Evaluation involves observation; observation comes with practice. Do not get discouraged if you are not seeing as much as you expect to. Keep practicing!

CHAPTER 9
ASSESSING YOUR TEACHING PERFORMANCE

pp. 90–102

<u>OBJECTIVE</u>

After reading Chapter 9 of *Children Moving* for the second time, you should be able to answer these questions and complete the activities related to assessing your teaching performance.

<u>READING COMPREHENSION QUESTIONS</u>

1. In what three ways can self-evaluation be implemented by a teacher? What kinds of data can be obtained from each method?

2. Identify two techniques of self-evaluation that you can use by yourself. What information can you obtain from each?

3. When would you want to use written instruments?

4. Of what use is it to know the pathway you traveled during class?

5. What kind of analysis can be made of student-teacher instructions?

6. How does the combined feedback and practice checklist work?

7. What is duration recording? What categories does it contain? How is each defined?

8. How does a duration recording system work?

9. What are support groups? Of what value are they?

USING YOUR HEAD

1. Why is accurate and relevant feedback necessary to help one become a truly effective teacher?

2. Why, in physical education, would one want to assess practice opportunities?

3. What information does a combined feedback and practice checklist give you as a teacher?

4. What is meant by "systematically assessing" one's teaching?

FIELD ACTIVITIES

1. Take a tape recorder with you to any class one day. Record the entire class session. Try to answer the following questions. (Preferably, the class should not be a straight lecture class; ideally, it should be a physical education class that you have received permission to visit.)

   a. Did the teacher spend most of the period talking to groups, to individuals, or to the entire class?
   b. Could you hear the teacher?
   c. Was the teacher's message clear?
   d. Were there mostly positive or negative comments from students? No feedback at all? Nags?
   e. Did the teacher always talk to the same students or address the entire class?

2. Observe a physical education class, some other class, or a supervised playground for fifteen or twenty minutes. Fill in the accompanying interaction checklist (see page 53). (You will probably not know many students' names; so identify them in some other way.) Check page 94 of *Children Moving* if you need help.

3. The opportunity to practice is vital in physical education. Observe either a physical education class or a recreation setting and record each child's practice opportunity. Use the accompanying form (see page 54). Again, you will have to identify each child in some way. Check page 95 of *Children Moving* if you need help.

4. A duration recording system is presented on page 55. After you have gained reliability with it (to gain reliability, you need to practice with others and compare answers until you observe the same thing at least 80 percent of the time), go out to a situation of your choice— physical education class, recreation, or adapted physical education— and gather the information on the teacher. Make sure you ask the teacher's permission first.

INTERACTION CHECKLIST

Situation observed:_____

Date:_____

Time:_____

Types of Interaction

Children's Names	Talked To	Smiled At	Touched

Teacher:_____   Observer:_____

Theme:_____   Date:_____

Situation:_____

OBSERVATIONAL DATA

Practice Opportunities

Children's Names				

STUDENT TIME ALLOTMENT IN CLASS*

Duration Recording System

Teacher:_____ Date:_____ Grade:_____

Observer:_____ Activity:_____

Number in class:_____ Time started:_____ Time finished:_____

Total time:_____

```
0        1        2        3        4        5        6        7        8
|TTT|TTT|TTT|TTT|TTT|TTT|TTT|TTT|TTT|TTT|TTT|TTT|TTT|TTT|TTT|TTT|

         9       10       11       12       13       14       15      16
|TTT|TTT|TTT|TTT|TTT|TTT|TTT|TTT|TTT|TTT|TTT|TTT|TTT|TTT|TTT|TTT|

        17       18       19       20       21       22       23      24
|TTT|TTT|TTT|TTT|TTT|TTT|TTT|TTT|TTT|TTT|TTT|TTT|TTT|TTT|TTT|TTT|

        25       26       27       28       29       30       31      32
|TTT|TTT|TTT|TTT|TTT|TTT|TTT|TTT|TTT|TTT|TTT|TTT|TTT|TTT|TTT|TTT|
```

Time Analysis Codes

M - Management

Coming and going
Getting equipment
Changing formations

I - Instruction

Listening to teacher
Give directions
Demonstrations, answer
    questions about skill

A - Activity

Practicing a skill
A game when 51% of
    class is active

W - Waiting

For class to begin
For instructions

CALCULATIONS

Activity Time

$$\frac{\text{Total Activity Time}}{\text{Total Lesson Time}} \longrightarrow \frac{\_\_\_\_ \text{Sec}}{\text{Sec}} \times 100 = \_\_\_\_\_ \% \text{ Activity Time}$$

Management Time

$$\frac{\text{Total Management Time}}{\text{Total Lesson Time}} \longrightarrow \frac{\_\_\_\_ \text{Sec}}{\text{Sec}} \times 100 = \_\_\_\_\_ \% \text{ Management Time}$$

Instruction Time

$$\frac{\text{Total Instruction Time}}{\text{Total Lesson Time}} \longrightarrow \frac{\_\_\_\_ \text{Sec}}{\text{Sec}} \times 100 = \_\_\_\_\_ \% \text{ Instruction Time}$$

Waiting Time

$$\frac{\text{Total Waiting Time}}{\text{Total Lesson Time}} \longrightarrow \frac{\_\_\_\_ \text{Sec}}{\text{Sec}} \times 100 = \_\_\_\_\_ \% \text{ Waiting Time}$$

---

*Adapted from an instrument developed in the Physical Education Department, Ohio State University, October 1978.

SELF-TESTING ACTIVITIES

1. Design a written form to assess your teaching performance with a group of third-graders. After you have finished, see pages 92 and 93 in *Children Moving* to check your work. Then try to find an elementary school teacher who will let you try the evaluation system out on his or her class. Explain that you will share all answers and that they are strictly confidential.

2. In the field activities, you recorded practice opportunities and feedback separately. Now, using the practice feedback chart on page 57, try to record both at the same time.

3. Using the duration recording system reproduced on page 58, observe three elementary or university physical education classes, recreation experiences, and adapted physical education experiences. After you have collected your data, make some general statements about how time was used in each class.

4. *Children Moving* suggests recording the pathways a teacher uses during class, but it does not include an instrument for doing so. With a peer, design an instrument to record a teacher's pathways. You may want to check the instruments used in this chapter and in Chapter 7 to get some ideas. After you have finished, get together with two or three other groups and compare instruments. Have fun!

PRACTICE FEEDBACK

Date:_____

Teacher:_____   Observer:_____

Theme of lesson:_____

Observational Data

Children's Names	Practice Opportunities				Teacher Feedback Movement Behavior			
					Positive	Negative	Positive	Negative

STUDENT TIME ALLOTMENT IN CLASS*
Duration Recording System

Teacher:_____ Date:_____ Grade:_____

Observer:_____ Activity:_____

Number in class:_____ Time started:_____ Time finished:_____

Total time:_____

Time Analysis Codes

M – Management

Coming and going
Getting equipment
Changing formations

I – Instruction

Listening to teacher
Give directions
Demonstrations, answer
   questions about skill

A – Activity

Practicing a skill
A game when 51% of
   class is active

W – Waiting

For class to begin
For instructions

CALCULATIONS

Activity Time

$$\frac{\text{Total Activity Time}}{\text{Total Lesson Time}} \longrightarrow \frac{\underline{\qquad}\text{Sec}}{\qquad\text{Sec}} \times 100 = \underline{\qquad}\% \text{ Activity Time}$$

Management Time

$$\frac{\text{Total Management Time}}{\text{Total Lesson Time}} \longrightarrow \frac{\underline{\qquad}\text{Sec}}{\qquad\text{Sec}} \times 100 = \underline{\qquad}\% \text{ Management Time}$$

Instruction Time

$$\frac{\text{Total Instruction Time}}{\text{Total Lesson Time}} \longrightarrow \frac{\underline{\qquad}\text{Sec}}{\qquad\text{Sec}} \times 100 = \underline{\qquad}\% \text{ Instruction Time}$$

Waiting Time

$$\frac{\text{Total Waiting Time}}{\text{Total Lesson Time}} \longrightarrow \frac{\underline{\qquad}\text{Sec}}{\qquad\text{Sec}} \times 100 = \underline{\qquad}\% \text{ Waiting Time}$$

*Adapted from an instrument developed in the Physical Education Department, Ohio State University, October 1978.

CHAPTER 10
DETERMINING GENERIC LEVELS OF SKILL PROFICIENCY

pp. 107–112

pp. 107–112

OBJECTIVE

After reading Chapter 10 of *Children Moving* for the second time, you should be able to answer these questions and complete the activities pertaining to skill proficiency.

READING COMPREHENSION QUESTIONS

1. What have we usually used to determine what would be taught and where in the school curriculum?

2. What have the authors proposed to use to determine what will be taught and when?

3. What are the four levels of skill proficiency?

4. What characterizes the precontrol level?

5. What characterizes the control level?

6. What characterizes the utilization level?

7. What characterizes the proficiency level?

8. What is meant by "task specific"?

9. Why is age not an indicator of motor-skill proficiency?

10. What are developmental stages of skills?

USING YOUR HEAD

1. Why are developmental stages of skill development helpful to teachers?

2. How can levels of motor-skill proficiency be used in teaching?

FIELD ACTIVITIES

1. Find children playing in any situation. Observe at least five children and try to assess their level of skill proficiency. Refer to the chart on page 110 of *Children Moving* if you need help.

Skill Observed	Level of Proficiency
Child 1	
Child 2	
Child 3	
Child 4	
Child 5	

2. Go to a local elementary school or playground and watch a group of children at play or in physical education class. What dominant level of skill proficiency do you see? Try to observe four groups of children. Don't be too surprised!

	Skill Proficiency Level
Group 1	
Group 2	
Group 3	
Group 4	

3. Find one child or classmate and have him or her perform three different skills (such as play tennis, dribble a basketball, and do a headstand). Assess skill proficiency in relation to each task.

Skill Proficiency

Task 1

Task 2

Task 3

SELF-TESTING ACTIVITIES

1. Without help, go to a university or local recreation facility. Iden-
    tify five individuals and assess the level of skill proficiency of each
    one. Record your comments, explaining why you made the choice you did.
    After you have finished, see page 110 of *Children Moving* and check your
    assessment.

	Skill Proficiency Level	Comments
Person 1		
Person 2		
Person 3		
Person 4		
Person 5		

---

2. Think of ten activities that you have participated in or have thought
    about participating in and assess your own level of skill proficiency
    in each. After you have finished, actually take part in five of the
    activities with a friend or group of friends from class and have them
    check your assessment.

Activity	Personal Assessment	Outside Assessment	Name and Date
1.			
2.			
3.			
4.			
5.			
6.			
7.			
8.			
9.			
10.			

3. Go back to field activity 1 and make a brief statement about teaching each person. What did you discover about each child's skill proficiency?

Child 1: _____

_____

Child 2: _____

_____

Child 3: _____

_____

Child 4: _____

_____

Child 5: _____

_____

CHAPTER 11
TEACHING GAMES

pp. 113–122

<u>OBJECTIVE</u>

After reading Chapter 11 of *Children Moving* for the second time, you should be able to answer these questions and complete the activities pertaining to the role of games playing in an elementary physical education curriculum and begin to develop ideas of how you would use games experiences.

<u>READING COMPREHENSION QUESTIONS</u>

1. What is the difference between games and sports?

2. What three types of experiences are games organized into? Define the purpose of each.

3. What happens when we place children in dynamic situations before they are ready?

4. When is it appropriate to move children from a static to a dynamic situation? Why is such movement necessary?

5. How are situations that require children to use games skills different from actual games?

6. What two things are attempted with games-playing experiences?

7. What is one difference between a games-playing lesson and a skill development lesson? What role should a teacher take in each?

8. Identify five types of lesson designs used to structure games-playing experiences. What are the advantages and disadvantages of each type?

9. What abilities do teachers need to possess to design their own games?

10. How does the teacher's role change in each of the five lesson designs for games-playing experiences?

11. How can teachers facilitate the development of child-designed games?

USING YOUR HEAD

1. Why are games easy to teach and require little intervention after the basic concepts have been understood?

2. What is the major purpose in teaching games and how may it be accomplished?

3. Why should children be exposed to a variety of experiences during game-skill experiences?

4. How can we provide for the variety of attitudes that emerge during competition and games playing?

5. Why would a teacher want to modify a predesigned game? How is such a change made?

6. What do predesigned, modified, and teacher-designed games have in common? How do they relate to child responsibility?

7. Which game design is best?

8. What is the meaning of the author's comments about adult games for children on page 121 of *Children Moving*?

9. How does a teacher progress to the stage of encouraging children to design their own games?

FIELD ACTIVITIES

1. Observe an elementary physical education class that is playing a game.
    Use the accompanying chart to keep track of the number of times the
    teacher stops the game for any reason. The notation can be in the form
    of a tally. At the same time, observe *one* child for the entire period
    and record the actual amount of time he or she spent in activity. This
    can be done quite easily by using a stopwatch and letting it run while
    the child is active and stopping it when he or she is inactive. Keep
    an accumulative record of time (start, stop, start, stop). Never erase.
    (Activity time is defined as the time the child is actually physically
    involved in moving in relation to the game.)

Number of Times Game Stopped	Time
	Total class time: _____
	Beginning: _____
	End: _____
	Activity time: _____

2. Observe five different elementary physical education classes and record
    what type of lesson was occurring when you observed. This need be only
    a tally.

    Invariant game skills: _____

    Dynamic game skills: _____

    Games-playing experiences: _____

        Predesigned: _____

        Modified predesigned: _____

        Teacher-designed: _____

        Teacher-child-designed: _____

        Child-designed: _____

3. In your neighborhood, watch at least five groups of children at play. Record what each group is playing, how many individuals are playing, what equipment is used, the number on each team, and whether you can ascertain any rules.

	Game	Equipment	Number	Number on Side	Rules
1.					
2.					
3.					
4.					
5.					

4. Watch at least five groups of children at play in an unorganized setting. Record whether each group keeps score and, if so, how.

	Score Kept?	How?
Group 1		
Group 2		
Group 3		
Group 4		
Group 5		

SELF-TESTING ACTIVITIES

1. All work begins with invariant games experiences. Working with the
   skill theme of throwing, design three invariant games experiences.
   Any movement concept may be used.

   a. _____

      _____

   b. _____

      _____

   c. _____

      _____

   After you have finished, check to see that the task (1) would be iden-
   tical each time the child repeated it (that is, there are no extraneous
   factors to change the situation) and (2) focuses on a specific skill.

2. The step beyond invariant games experiences is dynamic games experiences. For practice, change all the activities in question 1 to dynamic
   games experiences.

   a. _____

      _____

   b. _____

      _____

   c. _____

      _____

   After you have finished, check to see that (1) the situation changes or
   has the potential to change each time and (2) there is no competitive
   focus to the situation.

3. Choose any skill theme and find or design an accompanying game for each
   of the five types of games lessons.

   Skill theme: _____

   Predesigned game: _____

   Modified predesigned game: _____

   Teacher-designed game: _____

Teacher-child-designed game: _____
     (structure only)

Child-designed game: _____
  (structure only)

After you have finished, refer to *Children Moving* and check what you have designed against the criteria for each game.

4. Refer to field activities 3 and 4. What implications can you make about children's games from what you observed?

CHAPTER 12
TEACHING DANCE

pp. 123–138

<u>OBJECTIVE</u>

After reading Chapter 12 of *Children Moving* for the second time, you should be able to answer these questions and complete the activities related to teaching dance in the elementary school.

<u>READING COMPREHENSION QUESTIONS</u>

1. What should dance in the elementary school provide for children?

2. Identify two dance forms. Where does each fit into a curriculum and why?

3. What skill themes and movement concepts generally appear in dance content?

4. What is the focus of expressive dance?

5. What is the role of imagery in dance? What must children possess before they can effectively use imagery?

6. Into what two types of experiences can expressive dance be classified? What is the primary focus of each and how does the purpose differ at each proficiency level?

7. What is sequencing?

8. What is dance making? What procedures need to be included in dance making?

9. How can dance making be evaluated?

10. What cues do the authors give for starting to teach creative dance?

USING YOUR HEAD

1. Why is dance hard for many people to teach?

2. Define "quality" as it relates to dance.

3. Why is expressive dance more appropriate for the elementary school than folk dance?

FIELD ACTIVITIES

1. Review copies of curriculum guides for three different elementary school physical education programs. What forms of dance are taught and at what grade levels? How much time does dance occupy in a year's curriculum?

	Form of Dance	Grade Level	Time
School 1			
School 2			
School 3			

2. Try to find an elementary physical education class that is in the midst of a dance unit (this may be easier said than done) and observe the class. After observation, record the following:

Dance form: _____

If expressive, was it creative or rhythmic? _____

Major skill themes used: _____

Movement concepts used: _____

3. Go to a dance performance by any local or touring group. (Graduate dance recitals are usually frequent and the dancers would love an audience other than friends, family, and professors!) Try to identify for the different pieces performed the major skill theme and movement concepts. Notice whether each piece was rhythmic or creative.

	Skill Theme	Movement Concepts	Creative or Rhythmic
Dance 1			
Dance 2			

Skill Theme	Movement Concepts	Creative or Rhythmic

Dance 3

Dance 4

4. *Children Moving* suggests six procedures to follow when helping children make dances (see page 132). For one of the dances you observe in field activity 3, try to identify those six stages.

Purpose, idea, or theme of dance: _____

_____

Movements to express the intended idea or theme: _____

_____

Powerful opening statement: _____

_____

Series of actions rising to a climax: _____

_____

Climax: _____

_____

Concluding statement: _____

_____

SELF-TESTING ACTIVITIES

1. You have just been hired by a local school that has no dance in the curriculum. You feel that dance is necessary, but to introduce it you must have the approval of the principal. Outline the argument you would use to persuade the principal that dance should be included. Then check pages 123-125 of *Children Moving* to see whether you mentioned the major points.

2. You have been given permission to teach dance at the school mentioned in the preceding activity, but the children are not very receptive to the idea. Outline a general procedure for working dance into the physical education program. Include specific ideas you would use to implement the procedure. Check your answers with the suggestions on pages 133 and 136 of the textbook. Good luck!

3. The fourth grade is studying the American Revolution and wants to pro-
    duce a dance as part of the unit. This class has a good deal of back-
    ground and is quite cooperative. Use the following framework to help
    establish some guidelines for them to use while they develop their
    dance. Have fun.

    a. Purpose: to portray the American Revolution
    b. Appropriate skill themes and movement concepts
    c. Opening statement
    d. Actions rising to a climax
    e. Climax
    f. Concluding statement

    After you have finished, check the outline on pages 134-135 of
    Children Moving to see whether your work makes sense.

CHAPTER 13
TEACHING GYMNASTICS

pp. 139–149

OBJECTIVE

After reading Chapter 13 of *Children Moving* for the second time, you should be able to answer these questions and complete the activities involving the teaching of gymnastics in the elementary school.

READING COMPREHENSION QUESTIONS

1. Why are balancing, transferring weight, and supporting weight on different body parts fascinating skills to children?

2. What are the purposes of Olympic and educational gymnastics?

3. What two types of experiences exist in educational gymnastics? Describe each.

4. What activities are taught at the different levels of skill proficiency for both types of educational gymnastic experiences?

5. How are children introduced to equipment?

6. What considerations are there in teaching gymnastics?

7. Why is it important to vary the task in gymnastics?

8. Why is teaching Olympic gymnastics somewhat easier than teaching educational gymnastics?

USING YOUR HEAD

1. What is self-testing?

2. What is the difference between physical education and before- or after-school gymnastic programs? Why does the distinction need to be made?

3. What can be used in place of "official apparatus"? (Why does this equipment seem to function better in the elementary school?)

FIELD ACTIVITIES

1. Many of us have been brought up in an Olympic gymnastic program and find it hard to move from that to an educational gymnastic setting. This activity is designed to help you make that change. Pick an Olympic gymnastic skill that you are fairly familiar with, such as headstand or forward roll. Now try to analyze that skill in terms of skill themes and movement concepts.

Gymnastic skill: _____

Skill Themes	Movement Concepts
_____	_____
_____	_____
_____	_____

2. Observe a physical education class in a gymnastics unit. Record what tasks were asked of the children and how many of them could accomplish each task.

Task	Number Accomplished
_____	_____
_____	_____
_____	_____
_____	_____

3. Observe a gymnastic unit in an elementary physical education class. Record the number of times a child is spotted either by a student or by a teacher. This need be only a tally.

4. While observing in an elementary school, make a list of the gymnastic equipment available for use. How does this equipment affect the amount of participation?

SELF-TESTING ACTIVITIES

1. Take five Olympic gymnastic skills that you know. Analyze each of them as you did in field activity 1. After you have finished, pull out the elements that are common. Develop a general guide as an outline you could use to teach skill themes that are relevant to gymnastics.

	Skill Themes	Movement Concepts
Skill 1		
Skill 2		
Skill 3		

	Skill Themes	Movement Concepts
Skill 4		
Skill 5		

Common elements:

Skill Themes	Movement Concepts
_____	_____
_____	_____
_____	_____
_____	_____

General ideas that could be taught:

_____

_____

_____

_____

_____

2. On page 144 of *Children Moving* an example of a gymnastic routine is given. Develop four such routines (not in code) that you could give to children.

3. Gymnastic equipment is not readily available in many elementary schools. With a friend, brainstorm all the things you think could be used for gymnastic purposes. For hints afterward, check some of the pictures in the textbook.

CHAPTER 14
TEACHING SPACE AWARENESS

pp. 153–171

<u>OBJECTIVE</u>

After reading Chapter 14 of *Children Moving* for the second time, you should be able to answer these questions and solve the problems related to helping children develop a functional understanding of space awareness.

<u>READING COMPREHENSION QUESTIONS</u>

1. What is the primary reason for focusing on the concept of "space awareness" at the beginning of a program of physical education?

2. What is the meaning of "space awareness"? What are the characteristics of someone who is "aware of space"?

3. What directions in space are studied in this program? Why are some directions harder for children to understand than others?

4. How are the three levels of space distinguished from one another?

5. List the types of pathways that an individual might travel. What is the difference between a floor pathway and an air pathway?

6. Provide two examples of a large extension and two examples of a small extension.

7. List five body parts that you are able to place into a high level. List three body parts that you are unable to place into a high level.

8. What reason is provided for having children study self-space while they are stationary rather than while they are traveling?

9. What does it look like when children are able to travel safely in general space?

10. What does the term "travel defensively" mean? Does it relate to the speed of travel in general space? How?

11. When a stop signal is given for children traveling in general space, how can the teacher aid the children's understanding of general space by providing feedback?

USING YOUR HEAD

1. Why is awareness of one's space an important concept to master? Use practical examples from everyday life experiences to illustrate your answer.

2. The generic levels of skill proficiency are listed for each of the skill theme chapters (Chapters 17 through 27) but not for the movement concept chapters (Chapters 14 through 16). Can you explain the reason for organizing the chapters this way? (It may help you to review Chapter 2, "Teaching by Skill Themes," pages 13-21, before you answer this question.)

3. Choose a sport you are familiar with (such as football, tennis, gymnastics, or lacrosse). Describe how the six categories of space are studied (emphasized) in that sport.

FIELD ACTIVITIES

1. Observe a group of children at play and focus on their awareness of space. The accompanying chart (see page 83) will help you with this task. Focus on one child and on one concept at a time. Then focus on another child, but still on the same concept. One of the ways to gain information about the movement patterns of groups is by observing one child and then another. When you have completed this observation, you should be able to use the chart to answer questions such as these:

    a. In which directions did the children travel most of the time? Did they ever travel backward?
    b. Did the children travel in straight, curved, and zig-zag pathways? Or in just one pathway?
    c. How much did their play environment (for example, climbing on a jungle gym or playing tag in an open field) influence their utilization of space?
    d. On the basis of your observations, what recommendations would you make to their physical education teacher about the types of space awareness concepts that these children need to practice?

2. One of the keys to helping children operationalize the movement concepts is the ability to explain the concepts so that children can understand them. For this task you will need a tape recorder and a four- to six-year-old child. Your job is to discuss any of the space awareness concepts (except pathways) with that child, attempting to

Children's Awareness of Space in a Free Play Setting

	Use of Self-Space	Use of General Space	Direc-tions	Levels	Pathways	Extensions
Child 1						
Child 2						
Child 3						
Child 4						

explain what the concept means. Record your dialogue with the child (no more than five minutes long), and then write it out so that you can analyze (1) the child's understanding of the space awareness concept you attempted to explain and (2) your explanations and interactions with the child. An example of this task can be found on page 166 in *Children Moving*. It is titled "Mr. Jenning's Kindergarten Class Discovers Pathways." You will find this project very enlightening!

3. If you have already completed the previous project, the dialogue with a child, you have discovered that a visual aid helps children understand the concepts. The purpose of this activity is to prepare a set of space awareness visual aids. The task involves designing posters to explain each of the six categories of space awareness. These hints will help you design the six posters:

   a. The children are just beginning to read, so don't rely very heavily on written words.

b. The poster should be self-explanatory—that is, you shouldn't need to talk about the concept very long because the poster should explain it.

c. Children enjoy seeing photographs and pictures of "action" shots; they also enjoy seeing the art work of other children.

4. Children love secret codes. On page 144 in *Children Moving* there is a notation system that appears to be a secret code to many children. Let's see how good you are at solving secret codes. Look under the movement concepts section for the symbols for directions, levels, and pathways. Then locate the symbols for travel listed under skills—walk, run, leap, jump, skip, slide, and hop. Practice a sequence that includes at least three different locomotor skills combined with directions, levels, and pathways. Write the sequence down and then see whether your partner can follow it using only your notation system. If it's too easy at first, make it harder the next time. Here's one example to get you started:

Skill:

Concepts:

If you hopped backward in a curved pathway, you were right. Now it's your turn. Remember always to list the skill on top and the concepts directly beneath.

SELF-TESTING ACTIVITIES

1. You have just accepted a teaching job in a school that has never had an organized physical education program. You decide that the children need to develop an understanding of space awareness, but you are concerned that many of the concepts will seem too babyish for your fifth-grade class. For each of the six categories of space awareness discussed in this chapter, select the "idea for development" that you think would best meet the needs of fifth-graders. Jot the idea down and then briefly explain why you think it has the potential to work successfully. If you don't like any of the ideas in the chapter, don't hesitate to create your own.

2. By now you have no doubt discovered that it's harder to use words to explain the movement concepts than it is to use pictures. This task involves working with pictures; you may want to work on it with a partner. Your job is to make a collage (a mounted composite of pictures) illustrating the various aspects of space awareness. The best source is old magazines, especially *Sports Illustrated*. When people view your collage, they should be able to see all the space awareness concepts illustrated. Try not to rely too heavily on written labels, and don't hesitate to be a bit creative. Here's your chance to let your artistic abilities rise to the surface.

3. The purpose of this task is to design an obstacle course that can be used to "review" the space awareness concepts after they have been

taught. In your facility, you have the following equipment: tables, chairs, benches, hoops, milk crates, bamboo poles, ropes, tires, and mats. The first part of the task is to diagram the obstacle course, explaining how the equipment will be placed (see pages 225 and 231 in *Children Moving* for examples). Use the rectangular space outlined below. Be sure to explain the symbols you use.

Space Awareness Obstacle Course

Explanation of symbols: _____

_____

_____

_____

_____

_____

The second part of the task is to list for each of the six categories at least one challenge that will enable the children to review the concept and you to determine how well they have operationalized the concepts.

a. Self-space challenge:_____

_____

b. General space challenge: _____

_____

c. Directions challenge: "Can you travel over each piece of equipment in the obstacle course using a minimum of three different directions (for example, forward over the table, sideways over the beam, backwards over the hoop)?"

_____

_____

d. Levels challenge: _____

_____

e. Pathways challenge: _____

_____

f. Extensions challenge: _____

_____

CHAPTER 15
TEACHING EFFORT CONCEPTS

pp. 172–184

OBJECTIVE

After reading Chapter 15 of *Children Moving* for the second time, you should be able to answer these questions and complete the activities related to helping children develop a functional understanding of the effort concepts.

READING COMPREHENSION QUESTIONS

1. How does a movement performed at a fast speed differ from the same movement performed at a slow speed?

2. How does a movement executed with a strong force differ from the same movement performed with a light force?

3. How does a movement performed using a bound flow differ from the same movement performed using a free flow?

4. Initially, the extremes, rather than the gradations, of the effort concepts are emphasized. What is the reason for emphasizing the extremes initially?

5. When is slowness an important concept? List several movements.

6. What is the meaning of "acceleration-deceleration"? (Answer by using examples from *Children Moving* or from your own experiences.)

7. What does it mean to focus on the movement quality of an image rather than on the image itself? This statement will help you: "Imagine that the floor is covered with peanut butter six inches deep."

8. When do you change from focusing on the effort concept to focusing on how the concept relates to the performance of a particular skill?

9. What is the purpose of teaching children to apply the qualities of movement to their skill performances?

USING YOUR HEAD

1. Why do children seem to understand the concept of "speed" before the concepts of "weight" and "flow"?

2. What does this statement mean: "Any movement can be performed using any effort."

3. Select a sport with which you are familiar. Use the three effort categories to analyze the sport, focusing on the predominant types of effort required to play it successfully.

4. Certain movements are typically performed at one end of an effort spectrum—fast rather than slow, strong rather than light. Striking a ball with an implement is often characterized by a strong effort, for example. List six other movements (two for each effort category) and their characteristic effort. Try to list a movement for each of the six types—a movement that is typically bound and a movement that is typically free, for instance.

5. In a sport that features players guarding one another, the effort concepts are extremely important. Why is this so?

FIELD ACTIVITIES

1. Observe a basketball game. It can be a regulation game or just a game for fun played by friends on the playground. Focus on the three effort concepts and how they are used in the game. Which movements, for example, are strong or light? Bound or free? Use the accompanying chart to structure your analysis.

Observing the Effort Components in Basketball

Effort Qualities	Movements (Shots, Passes, Fakes, Guarding, Other)
Time	
Fast/Slow	
Sudden/Sustained	
Accelerating/ Decelerating	
Force	
Strong/Light	
Firm/Fine	
Flow	
Bound/Free	
Stoppable/Unstoppable	

2. Effort concepts apply to games, gymnastics, and dance movements, as well as to the movements we make every day. When you complete this task, you will have a better understanding of the effort components. Select ten movements that you perform daily (brushing your teeth, sweeping the floor, getting out of bed in the morning). Analyze each one by indicating the predominant effort qualities.

Effort Qualities of Our Daily Movements			
Movement	Time	Force	Flow
1. Getting out of bed in the morning	slow	light	bound
2.			
3.			
4.			
5.			
6.			
7.			
8.			
9.			
10.			

SELF-TESTING ACTIVITIES

1. Every day you hear a number of songs on the radio. Some of them can be utilized to help make the children's study of effort concepts more interesting (see Appendix 1, pages 485-488, in *Children Moving* for examples). The object of this task is to help you identify records that will help in your teaching. You may want to use current records. Or you may want to use records that you remember from "the old days." See if you can list at least one song for each concept on the accompanying chart.

Effort Concept	Title of Song, Artist, Record Company
Fast speed	
Slow speed	
Strong force	
Light force	
Bound flow	
Free flow	

2. Chapter 15 of *Children Moving* contains several photographs of children depicting different effort concepts. On page 178, for example, there is a photograph of a child exhibiting the effort concept of "strong force." Your task is to locate other photographs in the book (you may not use photographs from Chapter 15) to illustrate each of the six effort components. Include a brief explanation of why you selected that photograph.

Effort Concept	Page No.	Rationale
Fast speed		
Slow speed		
Strong force		
Light force		
Bound flow		
Free flow		

3. You have accepted a job teaching in a school that has grades one through six. The school has never had an organized program of physical education before. You decide that they need to develop a functional understanding of the effort concepts, and you plan to spend two days on each concept (a total of six days). Use the form below to outline your lesson, focusing especially on the differences between the way you will present the same concept to first-grade children and to sixth-grade children (see page 30 in *Children Moving* for an example).

Effort Concept	First Grade	Sixth Grade
Speed (fast/slow)	1. 2.	1. 2.
Force (strong/light)	1. 2.	1. 2.
Flow (bound/free)	1. 2.	1. 2.

4. Certain words seem to suggest certain effort. The word "confident," for example, seems to imply a rather fast, strong, free effort; "timid" implies a rather slow, light, bound effort. The list below contains ten adjectives. Identify, as best you can, the predominant effort implied by each.

Adjective	Time	Force	Flow
1. Droopy			
2. Greedy			
3. Prickly			
4. Bubbling			
5. Spongy			

Adjective	Time	Force	Flow
6. Floppy			
7. Springy			
8. Carefree			
9. Fierce			
10. Spikey			

CHAPTER 16
TEACHING RELATIONSHIPS

pp. 185–210

OBJECTIVE

After reading Chapter 16 of *Children Moving* for the second time, you should be able to answer these questions and complete the activities related to helping children develop a functional understanding of relationships.

READING COMPREHENSION QUESTIONS

1. List three examples of self-relationships, relationships to objects, and relationships to people (a total of nine examples).

2. What is the meaning of a "functional vocabulary"?

3. Define "symmetrical" and "nonsymmetrical" by listing examples of each.

4. In the game Simon Says, why isn't it a good idea to have children "sit out"?

5. What are the differences between matching parts, similar parts, and different parts?

6. It is recommended that you teach the concept of "relationships" with objects before teaching relationships with people. Can you explain why?

7. What is the meaning of "alone in a mass"? What is the meaning of "solo"?

8. Solo performances and intergroup experiences are not required; they are voluntary. What is the reason for making them voluntary?

9. Explain the difference between matching and mirroring.

10. What is the recommended size for initial experiences in intergroup relationships?

11. What factors are considered when making decisions about the most appropriate times to introduce the various relationships?

USING YOUR HEAD

1. Why is it important to discuss with children the feelings associated with competing against others?

2. Why do children need to be able to actually name a shape (such as "round") that they have made?

3. If someone who hadn't read this chapter asked you to explain why a program of physical education for children focused on the concept of "relationships," how would you respond?

FIELD ACTIVITIES

1. One idea for teaching relationships with objects involves setting up an obstacle course of elastic or regular heights (page 197 in *Children Moving*). Your task is to design and construct such an obstacle course. You may want to set it up in a room at an elementary school or on a playground. If children are not available, arrange to set it up for your class. You will need to follow these steps:

   a. Determine the location and the equipment that is available (chairs, tables, ropes, etc.).
   b. Formulate the appropriate challenges that you will use with your group. Don't limit yourself to the concepts of "over" and "under."
   c. Diagram the obstacle course.
   d. Have the students move through the obstacle course.
   e. Evaluate the success of the obstacle course by determining how well your students actually understood the concepts you taught. For example, when you challenged them to go under, were they all going under?

2. Chapter 16 lists three pieces of apparatus that you can construct— blocks and canes, hoops, and ropes. Your task (you may want to work with a partner) is to determine the least expensive way to obtain a set of thirty hoops. You might want to follow these steps:

   a. Determine the expense of making the hoops yourself. The Yellow Pages in the phone book will help you with this task. Be certain to figure the cost of the connectors.
   b. Determine the cost of purchasing thirty hoops by means of an equipment catalogue. Your teacher can help you locate a current catalogue.

c. Determine the cost of purchasing thirty hoops at a local department store.

d. List expenses for each source. Which is the least expensive way to purchase the thirty hoops? In terms of time, quality of construction, and such, which do you think is the best way to obtain the hoops?

3. Many games require players to move in relationship to one another while simultaneously maintaining an appropriate distance from one another— for example, doubles in tennis, the forward line in soccer, defensive backs in football, basketball players using a zone defense. (See page 207 in *Children Moving* for ideas for developing this concept with children.) This task involves observing players in a game that requires this spatial orientation. Choose from the previously listed games or choose a game of your own. Use the following format to guide your observation.

Observation Guide for Players Moving in Relationship to Each Other

___

Activity:

How the players move:

Recommendations to the players:
(stated in the form of challenges)

___

SELF-TESTING ACTIVITIES

1. One way to enhance children's understanding of shapes made with the body and body parts is to use pictures to show different shapes. Look through old magazines to locate pictures showing these shapes: round, narrow, wide, twisted, symmetrical, and nonsymmetrical. Mount the pictures so that they can be used effectively with children (you may also want to label some of them). While you're at it, see whether you can find some different types of pictures that your children will find stimulating—for example, abstract art, sculpture, line drawings.

2. Think about teaching the relationship concepts to a class of fifth-graders who have never been introduced to them. You feel strongly that their movement potential can be enhanced by learning these concepts, but you are concerned that many of the ideas for development are too babyish for this class. For each of the three relationship categories (self-relationships, relationships with objects, relationships with people), select the "ideas for development" from Chapter 16 that you think would best meet the needs of fifth-graders. Briefly list the ideas and why you think each has the potential to be challenging to ten- to eleven-year-old children. Don't hesitate to create your own challenges if you aren't satisfied with those in Chapter 16.

3. Using the "Guide for Reflective Planning" on page 99, write a lesson on the concept of "relationships with objects." This will be the first lesson the class (a third grade) has ever had on this concept.

GUIDE FOR REFLECTIVE PLANNING

CLASS NAME_____ CLASS SKILL LEVEL_____

LENGTH (TIME) OF LESSON_____ # OF MEETINGS PER WEEK_____

EQUIPMENT TO BE USED: 1)_____ 2)_____ 3)_____

4)_____ 5)_____

ORGANIZATIONAL PATTERN_____ FACILITY_____

MAJOR SKILL THEME OR MOVEMENT CONCEPT_____

    SUBCONCEPT(S) OF THEME(S) 1)_____

                           2)_____

IN THIS LESSON I WANT THE CHILDREN TO LEARN:_____

_____

       LESSON COMPONENTS   OBSERVATIONAL FOCUS

INTRODUCTION:

DEVELOPMENT:

CORE:

CONCLUSION:

LESSON EVALUATION (USE REVERSE SIDE)

<u>GUIDE FOR REFLECTIVE PLANNING</u>, p. 2

LESSON EVALUATION

    1)   HOW CAN THIS PLAN BE IMPROVED?

    2)   HOW COULD MY TEACHING PERFORMANCE BE IMPROVED?

CHAPTER 17
TRAVELING

pp. 211–238

OBJECTIVE

After reading Chapter 17 of *Children Moving* for the second time, you should
be able to answer these questions and complete the activities related to
helping children improve their ability to travel.

READING COMPREHENSION QUESTIONS

1. What components of traveling are taught in a program of physical educa-
    tion for children?

2. What is meant by a "naturally developing skill"? List two examples.

3. Is a fundamental locomotor pattern the same as a naturally developing
    skill?

4. List the fundamental locomotor skills that emerge from the walk-run
    pattern.

5. What is a mature running pattern? Do all children have mature running patterns? Do all adults?

6. What is the difference between a hop, a leap, a slide, and a gallop?

7. Describe the characteristics of traveling for each of the generic levels of skill proficiency (that is, precontrol and so forth).

8. What is orienteering? Why do you think it is increasing in popularity?

9. Describe how travel is studied at the proficiency level in games, in gymnastics, and in dance.

10. What is cross-pattern crawling?

11. How can a Tom Foolery rhyme be used to stimulate different ways of traveling?

12. What is tinikling?

13. How long will older children typically need to create a dance when they are working in small groups?

USING YOUR HEAD

1. There are eleven chapters on teaching skill themes in *Children Moving*. Why is the chapter on traveling the first of the skill theme chapters?

2. Running is a traveling skill that is used in many sports. List five sports and the traveling skills, excluding running, that are utilized in them.

3. Traveling to the beat of different rhythms is emphasized in Chapter 17. Why is it important for children to learn to travel to different rhythms?

FIELD ACTIVITIES

1. "People watching" is something many of us enjoy. Here's a chance to do it legitimately. With a partner, find a good location for people watching. Using the checklist "Observing People Walk" on page 104, observe the way different people walk (for a complete description, see page 212 in *Children Moving*). Compare your observations with your partner's. Can you draw any conclusions from your study? What are the implications for children's physical education?

2. Locate a child between the age of two and five whom you can work with for a few minutes. Demonstrate the traveling patterns listed in the checklist "Observing Children's Travel Patterns" on page 105 and ask the child to do them after you. Indicate whether the child can perform them easily, in a limited, uneven, halting style, or not at all. Don't worry about teaching the child how to do them; this task is simply to help you learn more about young children's travel patterns. By the way, be certain to obtain the permission of the child's teacher or parent.

OBSERVING PEOPLE WALK

Walkers	Bouncy walk	Excessive armswing	No armswing	Jerky walk	Duck walk	Toes turned out	Pigeon toed	Forward lean	Comments
1.									
2.									
3.									
4.									
5.									
6.									
7.									
8.									
9.									
10.									
11.									
12.									
13.									
14.									
15.									

OBSERVING CHILDREN'S TRAVEL PATTERNS

Travel Patterns	Easily	Limited	Not at all	Comments
Walking				
Running				
Hopping				
Leaping				
Skipping				
Galloping				
Sliding				

SELF-TESTING ACTIVITIES

1. Many of the ideas listed in the chapter on traveling are excellent for
    the introductory part of a lesson (see pages 32-33 in *Children Moving*).
    List two ideas for development from the traveling chapter that you
    might use with a class of children who are predominantly at the pre-
    control level (probably preschool or kindergarten), two ideas for a
    class of children predominantly at the control level, and two ideas for
    children at the utilization level. If you prefer to create your own
    "traveling" ideas, that's fine.

2. Review the diagrams of the travel patterns for the dance of Leah, Missy,
    Heather, and Sheri on pages 236-237 of *Children Moving*. Imagine that
    they are students in your class and write a response to them, reacting
    specifically to their travel patterns and providing them with addition-
    al suggestions (not requirements) about the travel patterns they have
    invented.

3. The "characteristics of water" are used as a stimulus for helping chil-
    dren to create a dance on page 228 in *Children Moving*. Use another
    example from science to create an "idea for development" similar to
    that on page 228. Don't hesitate to be a little imaginative in your
    thoughts: the children love it!

4. Music is an excellent stimulus for enhancing travel. For each of the
    following travel patterns, locate a record that will enhance the chil-
    dren's practice of that pattern. Use your own record collection, songs
    you hear on the radio, or the sources listed in Appendix 1 of *Children
    Moving* (pages 485-488).

Traveling Music

Travel Pattern	Song Title	Artist	Record Label
Walking			
Running			
Hopping			
Leaping			
Skipping			
Galloping			
Sliding			

5. Many of you have never had an opportunity to work with a group to design a dance. Here's your chance. With a group of from three to five people, design a dance that expresses a certain emotion or message. If you are having a difficult time, review the following pages in *Children Moving* and use one of those ideas (pages 132-135, 232-233, 234-236). These guidelines will also help:

a. The dance should be no longer than ninety seconds.
b. The dance should have an obvious beginning, climax, and ending (see page 132 in *Children Moving*).
c. Select appropriate music for your dance (see Appendix 1 in *Children Moving* if you need help finding music).
d. When you are satisfied with your dance, show it to someone—your teacher, the class, selected members of the class, a group of children. Ask them to tell you the message that was communicated through your dance.
e. On the basis of this experience, list at least three implications for teaching dance to children.

CHAPTER 18
CHASING, FLEEING, AND DODGING

pp. 239–256

OBJECTIVE

After reading Chapter 18 of *Children Moving* for the second time, you should be able to answer these questions and complete the activities related to helping children improve their chasing, fleeing, and dodging skills.

READING COMPREHENSION QUESTIONS

1. What are the differences between chasing, fleeing, and dodging?

2. Describe four examples of effective dodging movements.

3. What are the characteristics of each of the four levels of skill proficiency for chasing, fleeing, and dodging?

4. Rank the following tasks by placing the number 1 in front of the easiest (most basic) task, the number 2 in front of the next more difficult task, and so on.

   ( ) A defensive player in a football-type game pursues an offensive runner.
   ( ) Travel around the room. On a signal, change directions as quickly as possible.

( ) Stay as close as you can to your partner, who will try to get away from you.

( ) One team chases the members of an opposing team.

5. What is a fake? Provide several examples of when a fake might be used.

6. What is the reason for using large areas when introducing the skills of chasing, fleeing, and dodging?

7. What would you as a teacher look for when helping a child who is learning to dodge a ball? List at least three questions.

8. What would your observational focus be when you are teaching fleeing? List at least three questions.

9. When a child is tagged during a tag game, what is one alternative to eliminating the child until a new game begins?

10. Killer and Bombardment are games that have been played for years in elementary schools. What reason do the authors provide for not recommending them?

USING YOUR HEAD

1. The skills of chasing, fleeing, and dodging are typically not treated in books as a separate chapter. Why do you think *Children Moving* includes an entire chapter on those skills?

2. It is recommended that the skills of chasing, fleeing, and dodging be taught only after work has been done on space awareness concepts (Chapter 14 in *Children Moving*). Why has this recommendation been made?

3. Iona and Peter Opie observed that chasing games are often plagued with arguments and end in heated disputes. Why do you think this is so?

4. A friend of yours who happens to be an athlete picks up your copy of *Children Moving* and, after looking through it, says that chasing, fleeing, and dodging are naturally developing skills—skills that do not need to be taught. Present your argument that those three skills are learned, not naturally developing.

FIELD ACTIVITY

1. Several games are listed in the proficiency-level section of Chapter 18. Your task is to teach one of them to a group of children. (If you don't have access to children, a group of your classmates will do, but not as well.) Use the following form to list the skill level of each player and how he or she does in the game. For example, are players at the control level able to flee successfully or to tag others? Are they easily caught or hit with a ball? On the basis of your observations, draw some conclusions about why these are proficiency-level games.

Name of Game:				Number of Players:
	Skill Level			Performance in Game
Child's Name	Chasing	Fleeing	Dodging	
1.				
2.				
3.				
4.				
5.				
6.				
7.				
8.				

SELF-TESTING ACTIVITIES

1. List ten sports. Indicate which of them include chasing, fleeing, or dodging.

2. Children who are eliminated from games—from tag or dodgeball, for example—are frequently the children who need the most practice. On pages 248-249 of *Children Moving*, one alternative to eliminating children from a game is listed: when a child is tagged, he or she stands on one foot for thirty seconds and then resumes play. Your task is to invent five other alternatives to being eliminated. Try to make them fun. Please don't use laps or push-ups. We want children to like to exercise, not view it as a punishment!

3. Use the form on the following page to draw up an observation guide for chasing, fleeing, and dodging. List the specific components (observational focus) that you will observe for each skill. See page 81 in *Children Moving* for an example.

Observation Guide for Chasing, Fleeing, and Dodging

Children's Names	Chasing									Fleeing									Dodging								

4. After observing your third-grade class, you realize that the girls and boys need a substantial amount of work in chasing, fleeing, and dodging. In fact, most of them are at the precontrol level in fleeing and dodging. You make the decision to spend 5 percent of your lessons (nine days) focusing on those skills. Outline a sample sequence for nine days (see Table 3.3 in *Children Moving* for an example) and then schedule the sequence throughout the year, using Table 3.4 as a guide.

5. In the third self-testing activity you developed an observation guide for chasing, fleeing, and dodging. Your task here is to use the guide to observe a group of children. The easiest way is to locate a teacher who is planning to teach a lesson on one of the three skills. If this is not possible, go to a playground, observe children at a school during recess (with permission), or watch children playing in the neighborhood. You probably won't be able to observe all the children using all three skills, but do the best you can. When you finish observing, indicate the skill levels of the children and draw some implications about the types of experiences that these children need in their physical education program.

CHAPTER 19
JUMPING AND LANDING

pp. 257–285

OBJECTIVE

After reading Chapter 19 of *Children Moving* for the second time, you should be able to answer these questions and complete the activities related to helping children improve their ability to jump and land.

READING COMPREHENSION QUESTIONS

1. What are the two basic types of jumps?

2. A jump consists of three phases. What are they?

3. There are five different take-off and landing patterns for jumping. List them in order of difficulty.

4. What does a precontrol jump look like?

5. What are the characteristics of jumping and landing for each of the four skill levels? For example, what does a utilization-level jump look like?

6. What is the focus of the jumping and landing activities for the pre-control and the proficiency levels? (The overview of each section will get you started.)

7. Describe a low obstacle that children can safely practice jumping over.

8. What is the difference between a buoyant landing and a yielding landing?

9. Describe a sequence for teaching children to jump rope.

USING YOUR HEAD

1. What is the difference between an observation guide (see the self-testing activities) and a progress checklist for jumping and landing (see page 81 in *Children Moving*)?

2. While you have the textbook handy, turn to page 30. What is the meaning of the note directly beneath Table 3.3?

3. What are the major differences between stages 1 and 2 and a mature vertical jump (see pages 260-262 in *Children Moving*)? What are the major differences between stages 1, 2, 3, and a mature standing long jump (see pages 263-265 in *Children Moving*)?

4. List a minimum of five different activities that feature jumping and landing as one of the major skills. Don't forget various types of dance activities.

FIELD ACTIVITIES

1. The checklist on page 116 is designed to provide assistance to the teacher who attempts to record the progress of each child individually (see Chapter 8 in *Children Moving*, pages 79-89). It was derived from the progression spiral on page 259 in *Children Moving*.

   With a partner, decide what each item on the checklist (for example, "appropriate use of arms in jump") means. Don't hesitate to change the checklist if you feel items need to be clarified, added, or deleted. Then locate two or three children (be certain to obtain permission to work with them) and set up several jumping and landing activities that will enable you to check the progress of each child. Write a brief summary of each child's progress and what he or she needs to work on in the future.

2. Many subjects, such as reading and sciences, typically taught in the classroom can be enhanced through physical activity. This task is designed to help children practice jumping and landing and also work on their math. But first you will do the jumping and landing—and the math. Aren't you excited? You will need a partner to help you.

   a. Measure the distance you travel in a standing long jump.
   b. Make two more standing long jumps, for a total of three jumps.
   c. Record in inches the distance traveled in each jump.

   Standing Long Jump Data (continues on page 117)

---

1. Individual Jumps

   Trial 1: _____ inches

   Trial 2: _____ inches

   Trial 3: _____ inches
   _____

   Total _____ inches

INDIVIDUAL PROGRESS CHECKLIST

Skill Theme: Jumping and Landing

Children's Names	Jump down and maintain balance	Two feet to two feet	Run and jump from one foot to other (leaping)	One foot to two feet	Two feet to two feet over object	Hopping	Bent knee landings	Appropriate use of arms in jump	Balanced, quiet landings	Run and jump over low obstacles	Shapes while airborne	Jump to various rhythms	Use gestures while airborne	Series of jumps	Jump to catch an object	Jump to throw an object	Jump over high obstacles	Travel using a series of leaps	Jump and land appropriately from high level	Jump from apparatus to apparatus	Jumps on beam or bench	Jumping to mirror or match	Jumping and turning in a mount or dismount	Jumping using a spring board

Standing Long Jump Data—continued

---

2. Average length of jump: $\dfrac{\text{Total Inches}}{\text{Number of Trials}} = \dfrac{}{3} = \underline{\hspace{1cm}}$ inches.

3. Convert inches to centimeters and recalculate numbers 1 and 2.

   Then do the same exercises for the vertical jump. Jump as high as you can and mark a spot on the wall with a piece of chalk. Measure the distance from that spot to the floor.

   If you prefer, you can also figure class averages, but use numbers (not children's names) to avoid embarrassing a child who doesn't jump very well. It's also fun to figure how far (high) the class jumped as a group: "Do you realize that as a class together we could jump over the school building?"

3. One "idea for development" (page 274 in *Children Moving*) suggests that you have children jump rhythmically to the sounds of tools or machines (hammer, saw, axe, plunger, washing machine). Your task is to obtain a minimum of five different sounds that children might practice jumping to and record them on a tape recorder. Each sound should last approximately one minute. Don't hesitate to invent your own sounds—the wilder the better.

SELF-TESTING ACTIVITIES

1. You decide to focus on jumping onto objects and jumping over low obstacles with a class of children. You do not have enough equipment, however, for the entire class of thirty to practice the same task at the same time. Use the equipment list below and design five learning centers focused on "jumping onto" and "jumping over" (pages 45-46 in *Children Moving* will help you with ideas for setting up the learning centers). Use the blank rectangle to diagram your centers (also see page 298 in *Children Moving* for an example).

Equipment List

Vaulting box (1)
Benches (2)
Tables (4)
Low balance beams (2)
Milk crates (7)
Bamboo poles (1)
Cardboard boxes (15)
Blocks (20)
Canes (8)

2. The first step in the process of observation is formulating an observation guide (see pages 71-72 in *Children Moving*). Using the information contained in Chapter 19, formulate an observation guide for the skill theme of jumping and landing. Be sure to

    a. Distinguish between vertical and horizontal jumps
    b. Include observation points for the take-off, flight, and landing phases
    c. Understand the terms (for example, "Legs extend forward of body mass." "When feet contact the ground, do the ankles, knees, and hips flex?") before you write them down.

    Use any form that you think will be appropriate. You do not have to use the form suggested on page 76 of *Children Moving*.

3. One phase of planning involves developing a sequence of activities. This sequence is a guide that is seldom adhered to rigidly, but it does provide the teacher with an appropriate starting point. The sample sequence on page 30 in *Children Moving* was designed with an inexperienced class in mind. Your job is to change the sequence, adjusting it for an experienced class. The class is a fourth grade, and the majority of the children are at the control-utilization level. Last year they were exposed to the eighteen-day sequence described in Table 3.3 in *Children Moving*.

Dribbling

Skill level: _____

Rationale: _____

Task 1: _____

_____

Task 2: _____

_____

Task 3: _____

_____

SELF-TESTING ACTIVITIES

1. On page 426 of *Children Moving* there is a map drawn by a child depicting pathways and directions traveled while dribbling. If this child was in your class, how would you respond as the teacher? Write a reaction to Kelley.

2. Imagine that this is your first year of teaching. You have decided that you will spend approximately nine days focusing on the skill theme of dribbling. You have a third-grade class that has never had an organized physical education class before. Using the sample day-to-day outline on page 30 in *Children Moving*, outline a nine-day sequence of lessons on dribbling. Be sure to do it in pencil because you will probably want to change it once you get to know your children.

Lesson Focus

Day 1: _____

_____

Day 2: _____

_____

Day 3: _____

_____

Day 4: _____

_____

Day 5: _____

_____

Day 6: _____

_____

Day 7: _____

_____

Day 8: _____

_____

Day 9: _____

_____

3. If you don't already know them, find the rules for a regulation game of volleyball. Change the rules for a group of children. The following guidelines will help you with this project:

    a. The majority of the children have just entered the utilization level in volleying.

    b. There should be no more than three children on a side.

    c. Equipment and facilities are unlimited, so don't be afraid to dream a little bit.

4. It's a cold, rainy day and you can't take your children outside. Your school doesn't have a gym and the multipurpose room is already occupied. You have been working on the skill theme of volleying with your class. Using the "Guide for Reflective Planning" on page 153, write a plan for practicing volleying in the classroom. You select the grade level, number of students, equipment, and so forth.

GUIDE FOR REFLECTIVE PLANNING

CLASS NAME_____ CLASS SKILL LEVEL_____

LENGTH (TIME) OF LESSON_____ # OF MEETINGS PER WEEK_____

EQUIPMENT TO BE USED: 1)_____ 2)_____ 3)_____

4)_____ 5)_____

ORGANIZATIONAL PATTERN_____ FACILITY_____

MAJOR SKILL THEME OR MOVEMENT CONCEPT_____

     SUBCONCEPT(S) OF THEME(S) 1)_____

                            2)_____

IN THIS LESSON I WANT THE CHILDREN TO LEARN:_____

_____

LESSON COMPONENTS   OBSERVATIONAL FOCUS

INTRODUCTION:

DEVELOPMENT:

CORE:

CONCLUSION:

LESSON EVALUATION (USE REVERSE SIDE)

GUIDE FOR REFLECTIVE PLANNING, p. 2

LESSON EVALUATION

    1)   HOW CAN THIS PLAN BE IMPROVED?

    2)   HOW COULD MY TEACHING PERFORMANCE BE IMPROVED?

CHAPTER 26
STRIKING WITH RACKETS AND PADDLES

pp. 429–444

OBJECTIVE

After reading Chapter 26 of *Children Moving* for the second time, you should be able to answer these questions and solve the problems related to helping children improve their skill at striking with rackets and paddles.

READING COMPREHENSION QUESTIONS

1. Students at the precontrol level benefit from striking an object that has been suspended by a string. Describe five different ways that objects might be suspended for precontrol strikers.

2. What types of striking implements and objects are recommended for students at the precontrol level?

3. Provide two examples of striking with rackets tasks that would be classified as static or invariant (see Chapter 11 in *Children Moving*, pages 113-122, if you are unsure of the meaning of these terms). Change your two examples into dynamic (rather than static) tasks.

4. How does a teacher know when a child is ready to be challenged to "see if you can strike the ball on the opposite side of the body" (i.e., backhand)?

5. Describe the position of arms and feet when a child is striking with a racket or a paddle.

6. What characterizes each of the four skill levels (precontrol, control, and so forth) of striking with rackets or paddles?

7. What does a paddle facing forward (square face) look like? What does a paddle facing upward (open face) look like? What is the resulting reaction when an object is struck with a paddle held in each of those positions?

8. What does it look like when children "run around the ball" instead of striking it on the opposite side of their body? Describe a task that would help them learn not to run around the ball.

9. A child swings the racket so that it remains at waist height throughout the swing. What direction does the ball travel if the ball is struck too early in the swing? Too late in the swing?

10. What is the major difference between Wall Ball and Corner Ball? Which of the two is more difficult to play? Why?

11. Rank six tasks related to striking with rackets or paddles. List them
    in order from the easiest to the hardest. Be certain that you include
    at least one task for each skill level. Use a different striking im-
    plement or object for each task.

USING YOUR HEAD

1. *Children Moving* lists at least five types of rackets or paddles. Make
   a list of the rackets or paddles and place them in an "easy to hard"
   sequence. Explain your reasons for the ranking.

2. How long do you think it will take an individual to progress from a
   precontrol to a proficiency level of striking? State your answer in
   terms of "numbers of strikes" and in "varieties of striking situations."

3. Why is it more difficult to strike an object with a long-handled
   racket than with a short-handled racket?

FIELD ACTIVITIES

1. The purpose of this activity is to film the four different levels of
   striking with rackets. You will probably want to work in teams of
   three or four, for this is a time-consuming undertaking. The ideal
   medium to use is videotape because it can be erased and used again.
   If a videotape recorder is unavailable, the next best device is probably a super-8 movie camera. A graph check sequence camera (eight
   frames to a picture) is also very good. Probably the most accessible
   device is a 35-mm camera. If you use a 35-mm camera, you will need to
   plan to take a number of photographs of each of your four subjects.
   Where can you find the subjects? Start in your class, at a nearby
   elementary school or Y, or at the local tennis or racketball courts.
   You may have a friend or two who is at one of the levels you need. A
   little brother or sister can also be an ideal subject. Be sure to
   explain why you have placed each subject in the various skill levels.

2. With a partner, formulate an observation guide (see Chapter 7 in
   Children Moving, pages 70-78) for striking with rackets. (You may
   want to use the guide that you develop in the self-testing activities

portion of this chapter.) Go to tennis or racketball courts. Select four players to observe. Observe each player independently from your partner. Complete the following form for each player. When you are finished, compare your descriptions and prescriptions with those of your partner.

Observing, Analyzing, and Prescribing: Striking with Rackets

Player's Name or Description	Description of Movement	Prescription

3. The generic levels of skill proficiency are not age-related. They also vary from one skill to another (see Chapter 10 in *Children Moving*, pages 107-112). Working alone or with a partner, analyze your level of skill at striking with a racket. List three tasks that would help you improve your skill.

Skill level: _____

Rationale: _____

Task 1: _____

_____

Task 2: _____

_____

Task 3: _____

_____

SELF-TESTING ACTIVITIES

1. Formulate an observation guide for striking with rackets (see Chapter 7 in *Children Moving*, pages 70-78). The following form is provided to help you with this task. One example is included to help you get started. You may want to list more than three critical factors.

Observation Guide for Striking with Rackets

Critical Factors	What to Look For
1. The racket needs to make contact with the ball at an appropriate point in the swing—too early or too late will result in misdirection.	Is the ball consistently being hit to the player's left or right? Does the player consistently hit a certain type of shot (backhand, volley, to the left or the right)?
2.	
3.	

2. Intratask variation means that tasks are varied for individual children according to skill level. This is not easy for a teacher to do, but it is important because all the children in a class are rarely, if ever, on the same skill level (see pages 35-36 in *Children Moving* for a more complete description of intratask variation). Imagine that you provide the following challenge to an entire class: "See how many times you can strike the ball in succession without letting the ball touch the ground." For some children, this task is too easy, for others too hard. Describe four different tasks that you could use to vary the challenge for individuals. Indicate the level of each task. The accompanying form will help you with this project.

Intratask Variation for Striking with Rackets

Task	Skill Level
1. See how many times you can strike the ball in succession without letting the ball touch the ground.	Control
2.	
3.	
4.	
5.	

Hint: If you have been successful in establishing a learning environment, some children will be able to use different equipment, some will be able to work with partners, and so on, without distracting from the work of other children.

3. You are teaching in a school that does not have enough of the same type of rackets for every child. You have seven wooden paddles, seven nylon hose rackets, seven tennis rackets, and seven badminton rackets. Set up four learning centers for each of the four types of rackets (see pages 45-46 in *Children Moving*). At two stations you have wall space available. Use the chart on the following page to set up your four learning centers.

Station 1   Station 2

Station 3   Station 4

4. You have been working on the skill theme striking with rackets in an
    outdoor, blacktop area. Because of cold weather, you are forced inside
    to work in the multipurpose room. The children are ready to design
    their own games utilizing rackets (see pages 120-121 in *Children Mov-
    ing*). Describe exactly what you would say to the children. Keep in
    mind these items:

    a. Purpose of the games
    b. Boundaries
    c. Numbers in a group (and how chosen)
    d. Available equipment
    e. Rules ("Your game must include striking an object with a racket or
        a paddle.")

CHAPTER 27
STRIKING WITH LONG-HANDLED IMPLEMENTS

pp. 445–475

OBJECTIVE

After reading Chapter 27 of *Children Moving* for the second time, you should be able to answer these questions and solve the problems related to helping children improve their ability to strike with long-handled implements.

READING COMPREHENSION QUESTIONS

1. What is the basic action used in striking with any long-handled implement?

2. What is a sidearm pattern? What is an underhand swinging pattern? Which swings are used with which implements?

3. What is the purpose of introducing children to striking with long-handled implements?

4. What can be the long-term result when children try to swing implements that are too heavy or too long?

5. What are the observable characteristics of individuals at each level
    of skill proficiency in striking with long-handled implements?

6. Which diagrams of children striking with long-handled implements
    (pages 446-453 in *Children Moving*) depict children who are swinging
    with their arms rather than using their entire body?

7. Describe a mature striking pattern for striking a ball with a bat and
    with a golf club.

8. Why is it recommended that children initially practice striking using
    yarn balls or plastic balls?

9. What does a level swing look like when the player is attempting to
    strike a ball with a bat?

10. Describe two examples, one for bats and one for hockey sticks, of con-
    texts that are unpredictable or changing.

11. What does it mean to give with a hockey stick and then control the
    ball?

USING YOUR HEAD

1. Why are so many children fascinated by striking with long-handled implements?

2. Why is the concept of hitting a ball to "where players aren't" as important as hitting a ball to "where players are"?

3. Which of the long-handled implements discussed in this chapter is the easiest to strike with? Which is the hardest? Why?

4. What is the level of skill proficiency of most third-graders (eight- to nine-year-olds) in striking with golf clubs, bats, and hockey sticks? Do you think skill proficiency varies from state to state? From region to region?

FIELD ACTIVITIES

1. Volunteer to "build" a Whiffle Ball Golf Course (see pages 470-471 in *Children Moving*) for a nearby elementary school, recreation department, or youth organization. You will want to work on it with several other students in the class. The following outline will help you as you plan the project:

   a. Obtain permission from the school or organization.
   b. Obtain or make the necessary equipment.
   c. Design the course by visiting the facility before you actually set out the holes of the course. This will enable you to incorporate any interesting landmarks and such into the design.
   d. Be certain to instruct the children in safety before they play the course.

   Many of the students will not be at the proficiency level, but they will enjoy this experience, especially if you and your group emphasize self-improvement and enjoyment rather than comparing scores with each other.

2. With a partner, formulate an observation guide (see Chapter 7 in
Children Moving, pages 70-78) for striking with bats or striking with
hockey sticks. (You may want to use the guide that you develop for the
self-testing activities section of this chapter.) Go to a youth league
baseball or hockey game (the younger the better for this project).
Select four children to observe. Observe each player independently
from your partner. Complete the following form for each player. When
you are finished, compare your descriptions and prescriptions with
those of your partner.

Observing, Analyzing, and Prescribing: Striking with _____

Player's Name or Number	Description of Swing	Prescription
Child 1		
Child 2		
Child 3		
Child 4		

3. For this project you will want to work with a partner or in a small
group. Work together to make a videotape. Each member of the group
is videotaped striking an object with a bat, a hockey stick, and a
golf club. You will want to have from five to ten swings per implement—a total of from fifteen to thirty swings. You will also need to
decide on appropriate tasks for each implement (for example, hitting a
self-tossed ball with a bat or hitting a ball pitched slowly or rapid-
ly). Once the videotape has been completed, your task is to do the
following:

a. Analyze your swing with each of the implements.
b. Classify your swing into one of the four skill levels.
c. Explain why you are at the same (or different) skill level with
different implements.
d. On the basis of your own skill level(s), draw implications for
teaching children based on what you have learned from doing this

project (why children need more or less practice with different implements, how one actually learns to strike with different implements, and so on).

4. Identify a child who is at the precontrol or control level when striking with a bat, hockey stick, or golf club. (If you are unable to work with a child, a classmate or friend will be acceptable.) Organize three ten-minute lessons designed to help him or her improve the skill.

   a. Teach the three lessons.
   b. Include a copy of the lesson plans (see Chapter 3, pages 25-39, in *Children Moving*).
   c. Analyze your success as a teacher by describing the specific improvements made by your student.

SELF-TESTING ACTIVITIES

1. Formulate an observation guide for striking an object with a long-handled implement (see Chapter 7 in *Children Moving*, pages 70-78). The following form is provided to help you with this task. You may want to list more than three critical factors. Remember this guide is for use with only one of the long-handled implements studied in Chapter 27, not all three.

   Observation Guide for Striking with a _____

Critical Factors	What to Look For

2. You are teaching in a school that has a limited quantity of equipment.
    In fact, you have only five bats, five hockey sticks, and five plastic
    golf clubs. You haven't had an opportunity to make any additional
    striking implements yet, but you want your children to begin striking
    with long-handled implements. You make the decision to set up five
    learning centers. There are twenty-five children in your class (see
    pages 45-46 in *Children Moving*). List the tasks that the children will
    be asked to practice exactly as you would write them on the posterboard
    (see page 44 in *Children Moving*) that will provide directions for the
    children at each learning center. You will need five different sets of
    tasks for this class of fifth-grade children.

    Learning center 1: _____

    _____

    Learning center 2: _____

    _____

    Learning center 3: _____

    _____

    Learning center 4: _____

    _____

    Learning center 5: _____

    _____

3. Several games are listed in the utilization and proficiency sections
    of the chapter on striking with long-handled implements (pages 467-475
    in *Children Moving*). Teachers, however, are always searching for new
    activities for children. When one learns to modify and change games
    successfully, the number of games that a teacher might use increases
    considerably (see page 118 in *Children Moving*). This activity is de-
    signed to help you improve your skill at modifying predesigned games.
    You may want to work on it alone or with a partner.

    a. In another text, not *Children Moving*, find two games that focus on
        the skill of striking with a bat and one that focuses on the skill
        of striking with a hockey stick.
    b. Change the game so that there are no more than six children playing
        the game at once (if it is a team game, that would mean three per
        side).
    c. Use the following format to describe your games:

        (1) Name the game (you will probably want to invent a new name)
        (2) Objective(s)
        (3) Rules
        (4) Diagram (if necessary)

If you need an example, look at the game Six Player Tee Ball (page 471 in *Children Moving*).

d. Teach the games to a group of children (or to your classmates if children are unavailable). Have them evaluate the games and suggest ideas for improvement.

4. Children really enjoy the challenge of "navigating" obstacle courses. This task is focused on creating an obstacle course to be negotiated while the child is striking a ball (or puck) with a hockey stick. Use your imagination to create an obstacle course that will help children improve their ability to strike with a hockey stick and that they will enjoy playing. Your final product will be a diagram and explanation similar to that found for Whiffle Ball Golf on pages 470-471 in *Children Moving*. You can have fun with this one because you have an unlimited amount of equipment, space, and so on.

Hockey Stick Obstacle Course

5. Regulation softball is a game enjoyed by millions. The obvious fact, however, is that it is not a very good game for children who are learning to strike a ball with a bat, because there are so few opportunities to bat in a game. Your task is to modify regulation softball so that children have many opportunities to practice batting. Use the following format in changing the game:

a. Objective
b. Rules (consider the number of players, number of opportunities to bat, number of balls and bats, modifications of the play space, and so forth)

The more opportunities the children have to practice batting, the better the game!

CHAPTER 28
PHYSICAL EDUCATION FOR TOMORROW'S CHILDREN

pp. 479–482

<u>OBJECTIVE</u>

After reading Chapter 28 of *Children Moving* for the second time, you should be able to dream about physical education in the future.

<u>READING COMPREHENSION QUESTIONS</u>

1. What are some of the dreams mentioned in the chapter?

2. How do they fit into your vision of public education in the year 2000?

3. How can these dreams be accomplished?

<u>FIELD ACTIVITIES</u>

1. Make a list of the dreams listed in this chapter. Try to find out whether any of them is happening in any school system you know of.

Dreams	School System

2. Envision yourself for a moment as a physical education major (if you are not one). List the things you would want in a school that you accepted a job in. (Assume, of course, that you have your option of many jobs!)

SELF-TESTING ACTIVITY

1. Make up your own list of five dreams with regard to education. After you have finished, put it in a sealed envelope in a safe place. Five years from now, open it. Did the dreams come true? We hope so.